W9-BID-560

DELAWARE

DELAWARE BY ROAD

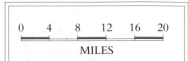

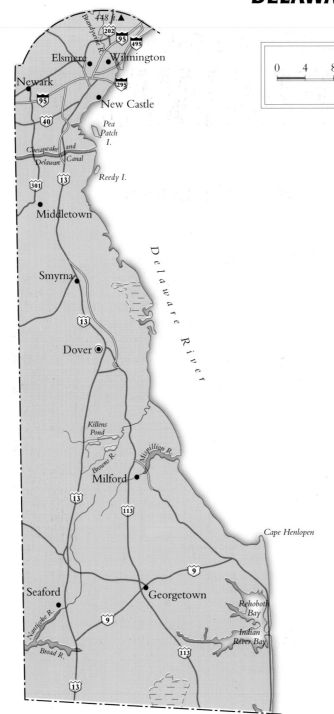

448 ft. ▲
Brandywine R.
202
95 495
Elsmere · Wilmington
Newark ·
95
295
New Castle ·
40
Pea Patch I.
Chesapeake and Delaware Canal
301 13
Reedy I.
Middletown ·
Delaware River
Smyrna ·
13
Dover ⦿
Killens Pond
Browns R.
Mispillion R.
Milford ·
13
113
Cape Henlopen
9
Seaford · Georgetown ·
Nanticoke R.
9
Rehoboth Bay
Indian River Bay
Broad R.
113
13

0   4   8   12   16   20
MILES

CELEBRATE THE STATES
DELAWARE

Michael Schuman

BENCHMARK **B**OOKS

MARSHALL CAVENDISH
NEW YORK

ACKNOWLEDGMENTS

Many thanks to the following for their time and effort in helping me out in my research for this book: Carol Hoffecker, Norman Lockman, Deborah Haskell, the Wilmington Public Library, the Keene Public Library, Jennifer Hastings and the Delaware Tourism Bureau, Ruth Sokolowski, Lynn Paul, Asha Dodia, George Turner, Haneef M. Shabazz, Debra C. von Koch, Maurice Barnhill, Kevin Nielson, Carol Ann Dougherty, and Jenna Luckenbaugh.

Benchmark Books
Marshall Cavendish Corporation
99 White Plains Road
Tarrytown, New York 10591-9001

Copyright © 2000 by Marshall Cavendish Corporation

All rights reserved

Library of Congress Cataloging-in-Publication Data

Schuman, Michael.
Delaware / Michael Schuman.
p.   cm.— (Celebrate the states)
Includes bibliographical references and index.
Summary: Discusses the geographic features, history, government, people, and attractions
of the state known as the First State, because it ratified the U.S. Constitution first.
ISBN 0-7614-0645-X
1. Delaware Juvenile literature   [1. Delaware.] I. Title. II. Series.
F164.3.S38   2000   975.1—dc21   99-16626   CIP

Maps and graphics supplied by Oxford Cartographers, Oxford, England

Photo Research by Candlepants Incorporated

Cover Photo: Photri Inc.

The photographs in this book are used by permission and through the courtesy of; Photri Inc. : 19, 29, 54-55, 60, 72-73, 76, 102, 109, 113, 117. *Photo Researchers, Inc.* : Michael P. Gadomski, 8-9; Mathias Pooersdorff, 18; Douglas R. Shane, 21; Tom & Pat Leeson, 25(top); J.H. Robinson, 26; Joseph Nettis, 75; Brenda Tharp, 84; Joe Sohm, 108; Norm Thomas, 119(top); Nuridsany et Perennou, 119 (lower); S.R. Maglione, 121; Tom McHugh, 122. *Delaware Tourism Office* : 12-13,16, 22, 58, 62, 64, 68, 70-71, 78, 80, 82, 85, 98-99, 105, 111, 115, 116, 125. Skip Willits *Mktg.* : 23, 25(bottom), 69, 135, back cover. *Jerry Millevoi* : 28. *Henry Lea Tatnall, Landscape-Brandywine, 1883, oil on canvas,14 7/8X 24 13/16 inches, Sewell C. Biggs Museum of American Art*: 30-31. *Historical Society of Delaware*: 34, 36, 43, 51, 52, 90, 129(left), 132. *Archive Photos*: 37,39,96, 127, 129(right), 130. *The Library Company of Philadelphia*: 42. *Hagley Library and Museum*: 49. *Delaware State Travel Service*: 86-87. *Kevin Fleming*: 89, 124. *Corbis*: Richard Pasley, 94; Bettmann, 131, 133. *Negroe Leagues Baseball Museum:,Kansas City, Missouri :*92. *Delaware State Archives/State Photographer's Collection*: 116.

Printed in Italy

1   3   5   6   4   2

To my friend Steve Otfinoski

CONTENTS

DELAWARE IS . . . .

Delaware is a small state with much to offer.

Delaware "is like a diamond, diminutive, but having within it inherent value."   —John Lofland, poet, 1847

However, some outsiders fail to realize that.

"Mr. President, the gentleman who has just spoken represents a state which has two counties when the tide is up—and only three when it is down."

—John J. Ingalls, Kansas senator from 1873 to 1891, responding to a Delaware senator

Being small has its advantages.

"We all know each other, and if there's a problem, we can bring the people and resources together to solve it. This is why I say Delaware is small enough to work."

—Pierre S. (Pete) du Pont, former governor

"My operating premise in Delaware is that there are no secrets. The grapevine works very effectively."

—Irving S. Shapiro, former Du Pont chairman

In many ways, Delaware mirrors the country.

"I think Delaware is pretty much a bellwether of the nation as a whole. The Wilmington area has operated like a Middle Atlantic city. The southern part has operated like the southern part of the country."   —Carol Hoffecker, history professor, 1998

Delawareans are friendly . . .

"I walk into a restaurant, and it seems half the people say hi to me by name."   —a Delaware transplant from New York City

. . . and they are proud.

"There is a provincial attitude here and quite a few people have it. It's that you can't be a Delaware native unless you're born here."
                    —Deborah Haskell, executive director of the
                         Delaware Heritage Commission, 1998

Delaware is a little state that is little heard from. Residents of Delaware do not make news as often as those of such megastates as New York and California. Indeed, the only time many Americans have contact with Delaware is while driving for fifteen minutes on Interstate 95 through the state's northeastern corner.

What many outsiders do not realize is that Delaware is a wealthy state, but one that has poverty and problems just like other places. Within its tight borders are industry and seaside solitude, centers of culture, and romantic beaches. There is a bit of everything in Delaware, and Delawareans are happy to admit it.

1 DELA-WHERE?

A word of warning: don't go to Delaware if you are looking for mountains. This is not the state to visit if you love to ski. Delaware is one of the flattest states in the nation.

Do go to Delaware if you like beaches and gentle farmland. The state boasts some of the grandest beaches along the Atlantic coast. Nearly the entire state sits on the low, flat Atlantic Coastal Plain, which extends from New Jersey to Florida. Take a drive through Delaware and you will see a mixture of leafy trees, grassy lawns, and level farmlands.

The northernmost tip of Delaware is the only corner of the state that is not part of the Atlantic Coastal Plain. It is part of a region called the Piedmont, which is noted for its rolling hills and serene valleys. Yet even here the hills are small.

WHERE IS "DELA–WHERE"?

Delaware is a difficult state to locate on a map. It does not stand out like Florida or Texas. Delawarean Deborah Haskell says, "Some cynics call us 'Dela–where?'"

So just where is "Dela–where?" It sits about halfway down the East Coast of the United States. The state occupies the northeastern part of a stretch of land known as the Delmarva Peninsula. The name *Delmarva* comes from the three states that share the

LAND AND WATER

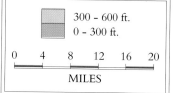

	300 – 600 ft.
	0 – 300 ft.

0   4   8   12   16   20
MILES

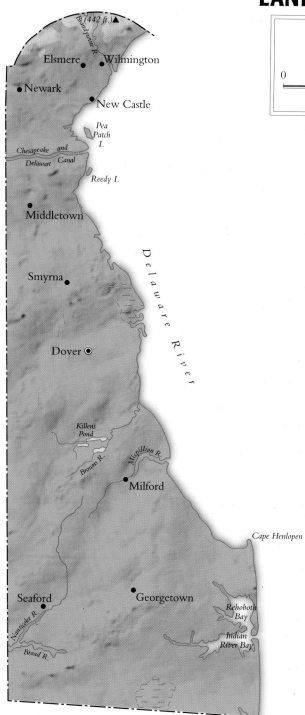

(442 ft.) ▲

Brandywine R.

Elsmere • • Wilmington

• Newark

• New Castle

Pea
Patch
I.

Chesapeake   and
Delaware   Canal

Reedy I.

• Middletown

Smyrna •

Delaware River

Dover ◉

Killens
Pond

Browns R.   Mispillion R.

• Milford

Cape Henlopen

Seaford   • Georgetown

Nanticoke R.   Rehoboth
Bay

Broad R.   Indian
River Bay

N
W   E
S

A LOW POINT

Many people consider Kansas one of the flattest states in the nation. However, Kansas's lowest point is 680 feet above sea level and its highest point is more than 4,000 feet above sea level.

That gives an idea of just how flat and low Delaware is. The highest point in Delaware is only 442 feet above sea level. It is near the city of Wilmington. The lowest spots of many American states are thousands of feet higher than Delaware's highest elevation.

Although there are some gentle hills in northern Delaware, the state has the lowest average altitude of all fifty states: roughly 60 feet above sea level.

Yet people who live here don't seem to mind. Those looking for mountain peaks can drive to nearby Maryland, West Virginia, and Virginia. And Delaware has something that states with huge mountains such as Colorado and Montana don't have: miles of warm, beautiful beaches.

peninsula: Delaware, Maryland, and Virginia. To the west and south of Delaware is Maryland. Below Maryland on the peninsula is a skinny patch of land that belongs to Virginia.

Delaware's northern border with Pennsylvania is unusual: it is a semicircle rather than a straight line. When the border was being set, it was decided that it would be twelve miles in all directions from the town of New Castle, so it is an arc. Most of the towns in this part of Delaware are considered suburbs of Philadelphia.

To Delaware's east is water. In the southeast is the Atlantic Ocean. The ocean water bordering east-central Delaware is sandwiched between Delaware and New Jersey, forming Delaware Bay. The bay gets narrower as you move north until it meets the Delaware River.

BIGGER ISN'T BETTER

The people of Delaware are proud to live in a small state. "We're small, but we feel mighty. We don't feel small," says Deborah Haskell.

How small is Delaware? In area, only one of the fifty United States is smaller: Rhode Island. At its longest point Delaware is just ninety-six miles long. Compare that to California, whose length is roughly eight hundred miles long.

At its widest point, Delaware stretches only thirty-five miles. By way of comparison, Texas's twin cities of Dallas and Fort Worth are a full thirty miles apart. The entire state of Texas, at its widest point, is almost eight hundred miles across.

Most of Delaware sits on the flat Atlantic Coastal Plain. This placid scene is along Route 9 near Odessa.

WATER, WATER, EVERYWHERE

Looking at a map of Delaware, one cannot help but notice the long coastline. Miles and miles of beach in southern Delaware are brushed and battered by the Atlantic Ocean. Delaware's beaches are a vacationer's thrill. The coastline here is wide and sandy. A smattering of dunes can be found, especially a bit inland amid pine forests. The biggest is the Great Dune at Cape Henlopen State Park. It rises eighty feet above the shoreline.

A lifeguard looks out over a deserted Bethany Beach, a rare sight in the busy summer season.

Along much of the southern stretch of Delaware is a sandbar that separates the ocean from three bays: Little Assawoman Bay, Indian River Bay, and Rehoboth Bay.

Farther north along Delaware Bay, the shoreline has miles of inlets and coves. Here are beaches, salt marshes, and national wildlife preserves. Bombay Hook National Wildlife Refuge is the biggest of these preserves. It is home to gaggles of snow geese, many other waterfowl, and even a nesting pair of bald eagles. Maurice Barnhill, an avid bird-watcher, says, "If I had to pick a single area along the Middle Atlantic region for bird-watching, Delaware would be the best. It's a small state, so the list [of birds seen] will not be as big as the lists of other states. But Delaware sits along the Atlantic flyway and it is absolutely superb for seeing shorebirds."

The state is also laced with streams and rivers. The most important is the Delaware River, which forms the New Jersey–Delaware border and empties into Delaware Bay. The largest river within Delaware is the Christina, a tributary of the Delaware River in the busy northern portion of the state. Bustling Wilmington Harbor lies at the mouth of the Christina. Brandywine Creek also flows through northern Delaware and empties into the Christina River.

Small waterways crisscross the rest of the state, too. These include the Broadkill and Mispillion Rivers in central Delaware. The St. Jones River flows through the state capital of Dover. While these three rivers all flow into Delaware Bay, the Nanticoke River in southwestern Delaware flows west through Maryland and into Chesapeake Bay.

One final body of water worth mentioning is Great Cypress

The lush forested banks of Brandywine Creek in northern Delaware prove that even this industrialized corner of the state has its wild refuges.

Swamp in south-central Delaware. It is the northernmost cypress swamp in the nation. As you might guess by its name, the swamp is dominated by bald cypress trees. The trunks of the trees, which flare out at the bottom, look like elephants' feet. One of these trees is known as the Patriarch Tree. It is fifty feet across, more than six hundred years old, and thought to be the oldest tree in Delaware.

Delaware state park naturalist Jenna Luckenbaugh refers to the flared bottoms of cypress trees as "elephants' feet."

Come here in summer and you will see what looks like green velvety carpet covering the swamp water. Some visitors think it looks like green slime. It is actually a plant called duckweed. In the fall the duckweed begins dying out and the pine needles turn a cinnamon-red color before falling off. According to naturalist Jenna Luckenbaugh, "The swamp is really nice for canoeing. You really feel like you're down in the Deep South."

HOW'S THE WEATHER?

Delaware's coast has a moderate climate. The ocean breezes cool the land in summer, and the warm waters of the gulf stream temper the winters.

In summer, thousands of visitors escape muggy cities such as Baltimore and Washington to enjoy balmy days on the Delaware shore. Kevin and Linda Nielson leave their home in northern Virginia to vacation on Delaware's beaches. Kevin says, "We

Broad and sandy Rehoboth Beach attracts visitors, both winged and two-legged, especially on summer weekends.

usually start going in mid-May. It's still cool but if you have a day when the temperature gets into the high eighties, the water can really feel good. The beach season lasts well into September."

Farther inland the summer air can be more hot and humid. In winter, snow and sleet are common. But compared to the states farther north, even Delaware's snowiest region—New Castle County, which receives about eighteen inches of snow a year—has a fairly mild winter.

PLANTS AND ANIMALS

Wander through the Delaware woods and you'll encounter furry forest creatures that seem more cuddly than fearsome. Raccoons, foxes (both red and gray), muskrats, opossums, rabbits, and white-tailed deer make their homes in Delaware. Among the many birds living in the state are Canada geese, snow geese, bobwhite quail, red-winged blackbirds, and ring-necked pheasants.

In Delaware's marshes and other wetlands, you'll see a huge variety of ducks, including mallards, mottled ducks, wood ducks, and pintails. Along the ocean and bay live shorebirds such as egrets, ibises, and herons.

Also residing in those waters are many kinds of frogs and turtles, including bullfrogs, diamondback terrapins, and snapping turtles. In Delaware's salt marshes one can encounter ribbed mussels and fiddler crabs. The state fish is the weakfish, which is also known as the sea trout, gray trout, or siderunner.

Delaware even has a state bug—the ladybug. Other insects found buzzing through the summer air or lolling on leaves include crickets,

Baby red foxes like this one make their homes in the Delaware woods.

The snowy egret with its toothpick legs lives among the salty waters and shoreline of Delaware Bay and the Atlantic Ocean.

Spread out like a fan is one of Delaware's more colorful animal residents, the wide-winged luna moth.

fireflies, and praying mantises. This little state also boasts the largest moths in North America. The greenish luna moth and the brownish red cecropia moth both have wingspans that can reach six inches.

It is possible that the wreaths you see on doors during the holiday season came from Delaware. The state tree is the American holly. Other trees found in Delaware are sycamores, beeches, yellow poplars, hickories, and oaks.

Beautiful, delicate orchids are among the flowers that grow in Delaware's wetlands. Violets, American lotuses, and lady's slippers

SOMETHING PEACHY

Georgia might be known today as the Peach State, but for years peaches were grown in abundance in Delaware. In fact, a hit song in 1915 was titled "When It's Peach Picking Time in Delaware."

Peaches are not native to Delaware. They were brought to North America in the 1500s by Spanish explorers. By the 1600s, so many peaches were grown in Delaware that people did not know what to do with them. Many fed them to their hogs as slop.

By the nineteenth century, Delawareans were shipping millions of baskets of peaches to distant markets by steamboat and train. The year 1875 was Delaware peach growers' most productive year: more than six million baskets were shipped. For the next forty years, peach peddlers throughout the Mid-Atlantic states were heard chanting the singsong refrain, "Here's your peaches, your nice Delaware peaches, your sweet Delaware peaches."

However, in the 1890s a virus known as the peach yellows began ruining the state's peach industry. Many peach growers lost so much money that they burned their orchards and turned the land into pastures. Some began growing apples, melons, and strawberries instead of peaches.

In 1890, five million peach trees produced fruit in the state. By 1920, that number had dwindled to 500,000. Peaches are still grown in Delaware, but the fragrant fruit is no longer king as it was one hundred years ago.

also grow in the wild here. Cattail and cordgrass thrive in salt marshes. Delaware's state flower is the peach blossom. It was adopted in 1895, when there were more than 800,000 peach trees growing in the state.

CHICKENS AND POLLUTION

Southern Delaware is covered with woods and farms. Travel here in farming season and you'll see row upon row of soybeans and corn. Most of this produce is used to feed chickens.

Today the chicken business is responsible for problems that were not considered when it was founded in the 1920s. It is one of the biggest polluters of southern Delaware's water. Farmers regularly use chicken manure as fertilizer. Rainwater carries nutrients from the fertilizer into Delaware's waterways, such as the Broadkill and the Mispillion Rivers.

The Environmental Protection Agency (EPA), the government organization in charge of overseeing air and water quality in the United States, is trying to combat the fertilizer pollution. It has announced a plan that would require Delaware's chicken farmers to get pollution-control permits to be able to conduct business. The farmers have been given a few years to find cleaner ways of disposing of chicken manure before the permit requirement kicks in.

Most poultry farmers are not pleased with the EPA over this. Kimberly Esham blasts the permit plan as "one more lousy thing we have to do just to make a living." A farmer named John C. Atkins insists that a few years is not enough time to find other ways of disposing of the chicken manure. Atkins says the EPA "is moving too fast. These environmentalists, if they shut this chicken industry down, maybe they can come down here and eat the beach sand. This whole industry has been here for seventy years. We're not going to clean it up overnight."

Delaware governor Thomas Carper has ordered research into

alternative ways of disposing of the poultry manure. One possibility is burning it as power plant fuel. Another is turning it into commercial fertilizer. A third is treating the chicken manure in some way so it doesn't harm the water. Hopefully, these or other ideas will allow both Delaware's farmers and its environment to thrive.

The wild grasses of Pea Patch Island brush up against the Delaware River.

2 THE FIRST STATE

A View of the Brandywine, by Henry Lea Tatnall

Do you know what it is like to have a disagreement with a brother, sister, or friend over a simple mistake? As a result, you may not speak to each other for a day. Then you apologize and all is well again.

The same thing happened in Delaware nearly four hundred years ago. The results on this occasion were severe.

A DEADLY MISUNDERSTANDING

For centuries, Native Americans resided in what is now Delaware, the Nanticokes in the south and the Leni-Lenape farther north. They lived in one-room bark huts called wigwams. Most survived by hunting and growing crops such as corn, beans, and squash.

In 1609, English navigator Henry Hudson became the first known European to explore the Delaware coast. But his stay was brief. The dangerous shoals of Delaware Bay caused him to veer north, where he would go on to explore and name the Hudson River in New York.

A year later, an English sea captain named Samuel Argall from the Virginia Colony was swept into Delaware Bay by a storm. He named the bay after Virginia's colonial governor Thomas West, whose title was Third Baron De La Warr. You can see how the name De La Warr Bay became Delaware Bay.

THE LEGEND OF SNOW BOY: A LENI-LENAPE TALE

Winter storms are common in the Middle Atlantic states, including Delaware. So it is natural that the Leni-Lenape have several legends about winter. One such tale is the story of Snow Boy, which tells of winter's good and bad sides.

Snow Boy was born a long time ago. When he was young, if he became angry at other children, he would grab their hands and suck on their fingers, which would become black and stiff. It was as if they were frozen from frigid weather.

One spring, when Snow Boy was old enough to go about on his own, he decided to leave home. He claimed that he had been sent to earth to help people track other creatures. He told his people that when snow fell, it was he coming to visit and the snow was his body in another form.

Snow Boy asked his mother to help him onto a slab of loose ice in a nearby river. Concerned that he might get hungry, she put a bark container of dry corn next to him. She then sent him downstream.

For a long time, the Leni-Lenape made an annual trip to the river. They took with them a bark container of corn to offer to Snow Boy. If a slab of ice appeared, they placed the container of corn on it for Snow Boy to eat. Then they would pray for his help as they tracked game.

Not until 1631 was the first European settlement established in Delaware. Near the present-day town of Lewes a small group of Dutch settlers made themselves at home in the New World. They built a fort and called their settlement Zwaanendael. In their native Dutch, that means "valley of the swans."

Settlers and Native Americans tried to get along, but a misunderstanding often had deadly results.

Their goal was to make money. A group of investors had sponsored their trip and settlement. The investors hoped the settlers could acquire earnings through trading with Indians and whaling.

As soon as they settled, the new arrivals placed a metal coat of arms on a post outside their fort. The coat of arms was a very important symbol to the Dutch. The Leni-Lenape Indians had never before seen such a shiny metal object. One young man was so fascinated by it that he brought it back to his village.

The Dutch considered this stealing. The Leni-Lenape man probably did not think the same way. Historian Carol Hoffecker says, "I think the Indians were just being playful. The Indian saw a tin thing that must have glistened in the sun and he was curious. The Dutch said the Indian who took it should be punished."

In order to stay friends with his new neighbors, the Leni-Lenape chief had the man who had taken the coat of arms put to death. Some Indians thought that was unfair. They attacked the Dutch settlers. Only one settler survived.

THE SWEDES AND THE DUTCH

The next European settlers had a more peaceful relationship with the Native Americans. In 1637, two Swedish ships arrived. The Swedes came with the same intent as had the Dutch: to earn money.

The Swedes settled along a river they named after their ruler, Queen Christina. They then built Fort Christina. In time, they chopped down trees to construct houses. These are believed to be the first log cabins in the New World.

But the Dutch were not yet finished with this region. In 1651, they returned to the area. They built Fort Casimir not far from Fort Christina. This began a fierce rivalry between Dutch and Swedish settlers.

The Swedes eventually captured Fort Casimir. But a year later, the Dutch recaptured it. Not to be stopped, they took control of Fort Christina. The Swedes never again held power in the area.

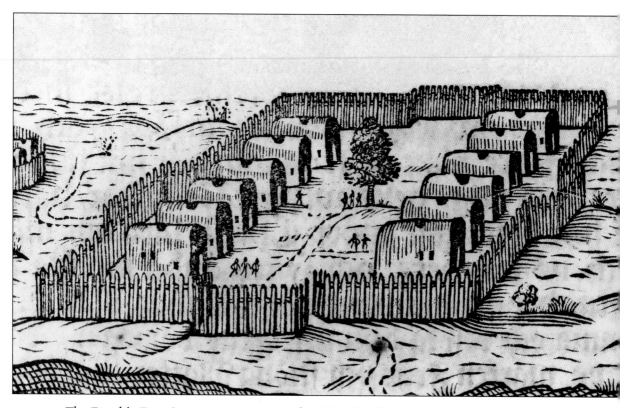

The Dutch's Fort Casimir, near present-day New Castle, was built just four miles downriver from the Swedes' Fort Christina.

While the Swedes and Dutch were fighting over this territory, England was watching the action closely. By the mid-1600s, the English controlled most of the colonies on the eastern seaboard. Delaware was one slice of land they were missing. With its access to water, Delaware was very tempting.

In 1664, the English sailed down from New York and captured Delaware. Then in 1681 England's king Charles II granted colonist William Penn a large chunk of land to the north and west of Delaware. He named it Penn's Silvania, which means "Penn's Woods." Soon it became Pennsylvania.

PENN IS MIGHTIER THAN THE SWORD

Penn belonged to a religious sect called the Society of Friends, or Quakers. Quakers are pacifists, meaning that they reject all forms of violence, especially war. Penn had hopes that Pennsylvania would be a place where people of all religions and backgrounds would get along in friendship. He made a strong effort to stay on good terms with the Native Americans. He once wrote to members of the Leni-Lenape, "I desire to gain your love and friendship by a kind and peaceable life."

Yet Penn had one problem with his newly acquired land of brotherhood. It did not border the ocean, and Penn wanted a route to the sea. So the British Crown gave him control of Delaware, too. Penn split his new land of Delaware into three counties: New Castle, Kent,

It was Pennsylvania's founding father, William Penn, who divided Delaware into three counties roughly three hundred years ago. The same counties exist today.

THE BLUE HENS OF DELAWARE

Although little fighting took place in Delaware during the American Revolution, the colony's men became known as some of the war's best battlers. Delaware's soldiers were legendary for their bravery.

According to one story, Delaware's fighting men killed time between battles by arranging cockfights. This is a sport in which two roosters (or gamecocks) fight each other. People bet on which rooster they think will win. Today, cockfighting is regarded as a cruel sport and is outlawed in many places. In the 1700s, that was not the case.

Delaware's roosters had a reputation as the fiercest fighters in the sport, so Delaware's soldiers compared themselves to the tough, disciplined roosters. Gamecocks whose mothers were blue hens were said to be the strongest. So the Continental Regiment of Delaware called themselves the "blue hens' chickens."

The nickname has lasted through the centuries. Today, the University of Delaware's sports teams are known as the Blue Hens.

Delawareans were lucky during the American Revolution. Very little fighting took place in their colony. The only encounter of note was the Battle of Cooch's Bridge, which was fought on September 3, 1777, outside Newark.

The British won that battle and soon took the young city of Wilmington as well. Within weeks, England's naval fleet was anchored off northern Delaware. Because of the risk of having the British fleet so close by, the Delaware legislature moved from New Castle in the north to Dover in central Delaware. Dover remains Delaware's capital to this day.

AFTER THE WAR

The American Revolution ended in 1783 and the colonies were granted independence. Now they needed a way to govern themselves. In 1787, delegates from the thirteen colonies held a convention and drew up the United States Constitution. Delaware was the first of the thirteen colonies to ratify (or approve) the Constitution. Because of its quick action in accepting this document, Delaware is known as the First State.

In the infant years of the new country, the people of Delaware spent their time doing just what people do today. They tended to their lives and jobs. As with most places then, the way Delaware residents made money depended on one thing: geography.

The three main elements of Delaware's geography were the ocean, the trees, and the rushing waterways in the north. It was natural then that in the late 1700s and early 1800s Delawareans built ships. And in the north, mills continued to turn wheat into flour. In 1785, a creative Delawarean named Oliver Evans invented more efficient automatic milling machinery. His inventions helped make flour even faster.

Another enterprising young man came to Delaware in 1800. His name was Éleuthère Irénée du Pont. Du Pont was from a wealthy background. His father, Pierre-Samuel du Pont de Nemours, had emigrated from France and became friends with such Founding Fathers as Benjamin Franklin and Thomas Jefferson.

The younger du Pont built a gunpowder mill on Brandywine Creek near Wilmington. In time he constructed more powder mills. This was a dangerous way to make money. Several du Ponts died

Men at work: these laborers are building a frigate called the Philadelphia *in 1799, during the peak of Delaware's shipbuilding era.*

in explosions. Yet when the United States began fighting England in the War of 1812, du Pont's powder mills served the young nation well and also put a bang into Delaware's economy.

THE ARTIFICIAL RIVER

A visitor to northern Delaware in the early 1800s would have been struck by the many sawmills, paper mills, powder mills, and flour mills. Wilmington also became known for its fine carriage and leather goods. A great concern was how to move all these products to places where they were needed. There were no trucks or trains then. However, there were steamships. The steamship in the early 1800s was state-of-the-art technology.

If you had visited Delaware in the early 1800s, you would have seen many sights like this placid setting—the Brandywine Mills and a mill pond.

THE BOMBING OF LEWES—1813

During the War of 1812, the British navy attempted to blockade the entire American coast. Lewes, situated at the mouth of Delaware Bay, occupied a strategic position, blocking access to Dover, Wilmington, and farther upstream, Philadelphia. On a blustery day in March 1813, the captain of a British frigate anchored in Lewes harbor and demanded that the townspeople furnish supplies for his ship and crew. He was astounded when they refused.

Words by Gilbert Byron

Music by Jerry Silverman

Dur - ing the war of eight - een twelve, A Brit - ish fleet sailed in the bay,

Trained its guns on old Lew - es town, Gave the peo - ple just one day To

furn - ish twen - ty bull - ocks, fat, Man - y hogs - heads of wa - ter, sweet.

Eith - er yield to the king's re - quest, Or to the guns of the

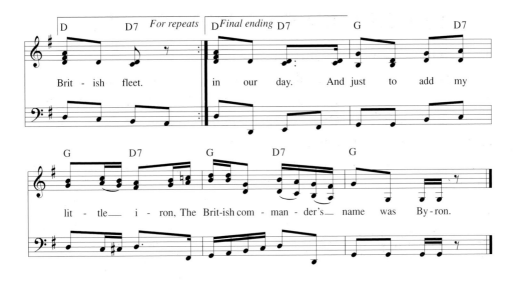

Brit - ish fleet. in our day. And just to add my

lit - tle___ i - ron, The Brit-ish com - man - der's___ name was By - ron.

Colonel Samuel Davis answered, "No!"
He'd never feed a British mouth,
And trained his little twelve pounders
Toward the big fleet in the south.
With that the British fleet opened up,
Two hundred and forty cannon boomed,
Solid lead screamed overhead,
Fire rockets whistled, shrapnel boomed.

But their aim was so atrocious,
After twenty-two hours of this squeeze,
A hound dog and a setting hen
Were the only casualties.
While the citizens picked solid ball
From the streets like manna bread,
And the little guns of Lewes
Gave the British back their lead.

And when the British marines tried to land,
The citizens turned them back.
Old men paraded with cornstalks,
British eyes were fooled by that.
They raised their sails so silently,
Slipped out of the Delaware Bay,
And they never came back again—
At least not in our day.

WALKERTON ELEMENTARY
SCHOOL LIBRARY.

And just to add my little iron,
The British commander's name was Byron.

Steamships sailing between Wilmington and Philadelphia had an easy route. They could simply travel the Delaware River. However, ships traveling from Wilmington to Washington or Baltimore had a long trip. They had to journey south on the Delaware River into Delaware Bay and the Atlantic Ocean and then all the way around the Delmarva Peninsula. They would then head north up the Chesapeake Bay to the two cities.

What was needed was another waterway like the Delaware River. So one was built connecting the Chesapeake Bay and the Delaware River. From 1824 to 1829, men with bulging muscles and craggy faces dug an artificial river, or canal, across the northern neck of the Delmarva Peninsula. It was called the Chesapeake and Delaware Canal (and became known as the C & D Canal.) This canal still separates northern and southern Delaware.

SLAVERY AND FREEDOM

Like many states, Delaware permitted slavery. In the Deep South, African slaves worked plantations. The region's economy depended on unpaid slave labor.

But Delaware was a different kind of slave state. It was a border state, located partly in the North and partly in the South. While some farmers in southern Delaware used slave labor, most Delawareans were against slavery.

Indeed, blacks in Delaware had freedoms and privileges those living farther south did not have. In Delaware, blacks were considered free unless it could be proven they were slaves. In the Deep South, the opposite was true. In Delaware, free blacks could be witnesses

TWO MOST DIFFERENT PEOPLE

The different viewpoints regarding slavery in the First State were summed up by two famous Delawareans. One was a woman named Lucretia "Patty" Cannon. For decades, she and a band of outlaws kidnapped free black men, women, and children to be sold into slavery. She was captured but died in prison awaiting trial.

At the opposite end of the spectrum was Thomas Garrett. He was a devout Quaker who helped more than two thousand slaves escape by way of the Underground Railroad. The Underground Railroad was not a train. Instead, it was the name for a network of places where slaves were sheltered while fleeing from the slaveholding South to the free North and Canada. Garrett's home in Wilmington was the last of these havens before slaves reached Pennsylvania, where slavery was outlawed.

Since slaves were considered property, Garrett was committing theft by helping slaves escape from their owners. He was found guilty of theft in 1848 and ordered to pay a heavy fine. Garrett had to sell his home to pay the fine, but he had no regrets. He said he would continue to help any slaves he could, and he did.

in trials. That was not true in the Deep South. In the early nineteenth century, Delaware passed laws making it illegal to bring new slaves into the state. However, no free blacks were allowed to enter Delaware either. That meant that some African Americans were legally unable to live near members of their own families.

THE CIVIL WAR

Finally, the issue of slavery came to a head. Abraham Lincoln of the new Republican Party was elected president on a strong anti-slavery platform in November 1860. Fearing they would lose the right to own slaves, several Southern states seceded from the United States to form their own country called the Confederate States of America. In April 1861, the Confederates attacked Fort Sumter in South Carolina. This was the beginning of the Civil War.

Although Delaware was a slave state, it stayed in the Union. Historian Carol Hoffecker says, "Delaware was mainly pro-Union, but some in southern Delaware were pro-Confederacy. Others felt Lincoln's war policy was wrong. They felt that if the South wanted to leave, they should be allowed to."

As it had been during the American Revolution, Delaware was lucky during the Civil War. No major battles were fought in the state. Perhaps Delaware's greatest contribution to the war effort was gunpowder made at the du Pont plants. It is estimated that the du Ponts supplied from one-third to one-half of all gunpowder used by the North.

After the war, Delaware had more in common with the Old South than the industrial North in its attitude toward black people. For example, a poll tax was passed by the Delaware legislature, forcing people to pay a tax before they could vote. Many African Americans could not afford to pay the tax. Those who could pay were often ignored by tax collectors. At the same time, many whites were not asked to pay the tax.

A GAME OF MONOPOLY

Over the next several decades, northern Delaware became a hotbed

The du Pont gunpowder works were the beginning of what would become an amazing industrial empire.

of industrial growth. Factories in and around Wilmington made steel, railroad cars, ships, and paper. And the du Pont family's powder works continued to thrive. The du Ponts were so successful that they had virtually no competition. That kind of situation is called a monopoly.

In 1907, the du Pont gunpowder business was sued under the Sherman Anti-Trust Act, which banned monopolies. The reasoning behind the law is that competition causes products and services to improve. Du Pont lost the lawsuit and had to give up some of its powder-making business. So the du Pont family decided to make something else: chemicals.

As with gunpowder, the du Ponts' chemical business was very successful. At the same time, members of the du Pont family were becoming active in state politics and were leaders in the community. By the early twentieth century, the du Ponts were the most prominent family in Delaware. The Du Pont Company was famous throughout the world. (Although the du Ponts spell their last name with a lowercase d, the company spells its name with a capital D.)

Perhaps Du Pont's greatest chemical invention was nylon, created in a Delaware lab in 1938. Today nylon is used in products such as stockings. However, in World War II, nylon was used in making parachutes, flak jackets, tires, and other war products.

TO THE PRESENT

After World War II ended in 1945, race relations became a major issue across the United States. African Americans had had enough of living under segregation (separation of the races). Though Delaware was not rife with segregation as were states in the Deep South, there were places where blacks and whites were legally separated. These included public schools, theaters, and restaurants. In 1952, a Delaware court ruled that segregation in public places, including schools, was against the law.

Laws and court decisions do not always change people's attitudes. School segregation, especially in Delaware's two southern

Dr. Wallace Carothers, a Du Pont chemist, developed nylon in the late 1930s.

counties, was not completely stopped until the mid-1960s. In the mid- and late 1960s, Wilmington was a prime example of "white flight." A large number of whites fearful of living with African Americans left the city and moved to the suburbs.

At the same time, blacks in Wilmington and other cities did not have the high-paying job opportunities that whites did. It looked as if they would never get those same chances. Blacks grew more and more frustrated and angry. Inner cities across America erupted in violence. A civil rights activist named Roger Wilkins once said,

Wilmington, like many American cities, fell victim to racial violence in the late 1960s.

"Generations of heaping inferiority into our souls needed to be purged. And if you're going to put that awful stuff into people, when people begin to expel it, it's not coming out pretty."

Riots hit Wilmington in July 1967 and after the murder of civil rights leader Martin Luther King in April 1968. As a result, changes were made in Delaware. A fair-housing law was passed, making it illegal to deny a person a home solely because of race. One of the boldest policies was called urban homesteading. People were given homes in poor shape free of charge. The only condition was that they spend money to make their house liveable. Observers say the program has had mixed success.

Over the last few decades, tourism and banking have joined chemicals and manufacturing as the state's biggest industries. Today, diversity, in terms of both race and the economy, is a key part of Delaware's character.

3 MAKING LAWS AND LIVINGS

The capitol in Dover

Don't look for anything unusual about Delaware's state government. The system is as typically American as blue jeans and the Super Bowl.

INSIDE GOVERNMENT

The way Delaware's government works is very similar to the manner in which the United States government operates. Delaware's government is divided into three branches: executive, legislative, and judicial.

Executive. The chief executive of Delaware is the governor, who serves a four-year term. The governor can be elected to no more than two terms. After the legislature passes a bill, the governor either signs it to make it law or vetoes it to reject it. He or she also appoints many officials including state judges and heads of departments.

Legislative. The state legislature is called the Delaware General Assembly. It is divided into two bodies, the senate and the house of representatives. The forty-one representatives serve two-year terms, while the twenty-one senators serve four-year terms. The Delaware General Assembly is responsible for passing and repealing laws.

Judicial. Like the federal government, the state of Delaware has

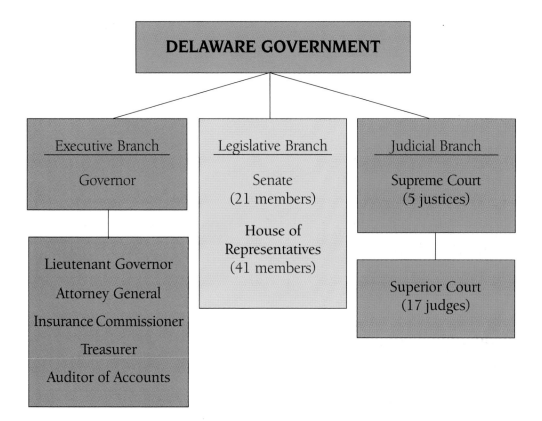

DELAWARE GOVERNMENT

Executive Branch

Governor

Lieutenant Governor

Attorney General

Insurance Commissioner

Treasurer

Auditor of Accounts

Legislative Branch

Senate
(21 members)

House of
Representatives
(41 members)

Judicial Branch

Supreme Court
(5 justices)

Superior Court
(17 judges)

a supreme court. Its job is to hear appeals to decisions made in Delaware's lower court. Delaware's supreme court has five justices who serve twelve-year terms.

There are several other state courts in Delaware. The superior court hears all major cases involving criminal activity, personal injury, and libel. The superior court also hears appeals from lower courts across the state.

The court of chancery makes decisions in matters relating to land sales, estates, and business disputes. The court of common pleas hears cases involving minor offenses or disputes between people.

A TRUE DELAWARE CUSTOM

Because Delaware is small, it can maintain traditions some larger states cannot. A perfect example is Return Day. It is a tribute to democracy and the peaceful exchange of power that occurs in the United States.

Return Day takes place two days after every general election. Its beginnings date to the days before computers, television, or even radio. Back then, citizens had to travel to their county seats to hear election results.

Today, upwards of ten thousand Delaware citizens show up for the festivities in the Sussex County community of Georgetown. In a show of goodwill, both winning and losing candidates ride together in a parade of horse-drawn carriages and floats through the center of town.

Following the parade, speeches are given and final vote totals are formally announced. Everyone then indulges in a bull roast.

In the evening, parties take place throughout Georgetown. Republicans and Democrats dance and socialize with each other in the spirit of friendship and cooperation. Even if they were not up for reelection, Delaware's two U.S. senators, its congressperson, and its governor usually show up for Return Day.

One would be hard-pressed to find such an event taking place in a huge state like California or Texas.

THE SAMANTHA CASE

One Delaware Family Court case that made national news in the late 1990s involved a ten-year-old girl named Samantha. She had been abandoned at age six by her mother who was a drug addict. For the next four years Samantha lived in four foster homes, including one in which she may have been abused. Samantha saw a counselor who helped her cope with the problems in her life. In time the counselor grew to love Samantha and wanted to adopt her.

Samantha sued to "divorce" her mother so she could live with her counselor. However, by the time Samantha reached age ten, her mother was no longer addicted and wanted custody of Samantha. The Delaware Family Court decided that Samantha should be united with her mother.

Samantha appealed to the state supreme court. National children's rights groups took her side and helped her make a case before the state's highest court. On June 19, 1998, the court ruled in Samantha's favor.

Within a few weeks, however, Samantha and her mother reconciled. Samantha agreed to move in with her mother, who lives in another state. Around the same time, Delaware governor Thomas Carper signed a law making it easier for children abandoned by their parents to divorce them. The new law forces the family court to consider if a child would be emotionally harmed if forced to live with neglectful parents.

Cases regarding family relations are heard in the family court.

All of Delaware's judges are nominated by the governor and confirmed by the Delaware General Assembly. Delaware's judges must be a balance of Democrats and Republicans.

A RICH STATE

Delaware is a wealthy state. Its workers have one of the highest average incomes in the nation.

The rich state got richer in 1994 when Delaware won an important lawsuit against the state of New York. As a result, New York owed Delaware $220 million.

What will Delaware do with all that money? Some will be used

Governor Thomas Carper said to the people of Delaware, regarding his state's $220 million wind- fall, "Delaware will use this once-in-a- lifetime opportunity to preserve our environment, revitalize our communities, and improve our education." Here, kids gather around a computer in a school classroom.

to improve Delaware's water and wastewater systems and to purchase more state parkland and build walking paths and bicycle trails. The money may also be used to bring the latest computer technology to Delaware's schools, improve the Port of Wilmington, and revitalize crumbling city neighborhoods, a process known as urban renewal.

One of the best examples of urban renewal is the First USA Riverfront Arts Center. It opened in 1998 in what had been a decaying section of Wilmington along the Christina River. The first major traveling exhibit displayed treasures that had belonged to the last royal family of Russia, who were forced from power in 1918. On view were items such as the Russian imperial throne and a two-hundred-year-old gilded coach. Before the arts center was built, this was the type of exhibition that would have bypassed Wilmington for a big city such as New York or Washington. Because of the arts center, people came from all over the Northeast and Mid-Atlantic states to Wilmington.

SLOT MACHINES AND HORSES

In recent years, Delaware has tapped into a new means of gaining revenue: casino gambling. In the mid-1990s, the state began permitting slot machine gambling. Many of Delaware's leaders, including Governor Thomas Carper, were against the idea. Some were concerned that gambling would bring organized crime into the state. Others believe gambling is sinful. Still others, including Governor Carper, were unsure whether casino gambling in Delaware would be able to compete with the big-time gambling

They're always off and running at Delaware Park, where 30 percent of the racetrack's gambling profits are given to the state government.

operations in Atlantic City, New Jersey, just a short drive away.

The state decided to permit casino gambling only at Delaware's three horse-racing tracks, where betting on horses was already legal. The racetracks had been doing poorly. They had not been attracting the best horses and were not living up to their potential as moneymakers. Gambling supporters thought that the addition of casino gambling would bring in more customers and a better quality of horses.

In terms of raising money, the experiment has so far been successful. The state gets roughly 30 percent of the tracks' profits from the casino gambling.

AT WORK IN DELAWARE

For decades, if you met somebody from Delaware you would assume that person worked for Du Pont. To outsiders, the du Ponts seemed to own the state of Delaware. Deborah Haskell, executive director of the Delaware Heritage Commission, admits that "for a long time that impression was somewhat accurate." It was basically a company town. Wilmington was known as the Chemical Capital of America.

Now things have changed. Du Pont has gone from being a Delaware company to having plants and offices worldwide. In addition, Du Pont, like many American businesses, laid off many workers in the early 1990s. Some scientists who lost jobs at Du Pont started their own chemical research businesses. Other long-standing chemical companies, such as Hercules and ICI, are also located in Delaware.

Today, many people who don't remember Du Pont's dominance in Delaware associate the First State with a different kind of business. They often receive letters in the mail with a Wilmington postmark from banks offering credit card applications.

Delaware's emergence as a banking center began in 1981 when Governor Pierre S. (Pete) du Pont signed the Financial Center Development Act (FCDA). It may sound dry, but the FCDA revolutionized the banking industry. Most states had limits on the interest rates banks could charge customers. The FCDA removed all limits for banks located in Delaware. Banks could now charge whatever customers were willing to pay.

A second important change concerned taxes. At that time in most states, banks paid one flat rate of income tax. Thanks to the FCDA, as a bank in Delaware earns more, its tax rate goes down.

Once the FCDA became law, banks from across the nation flocked to Delaware to set up offices. Since then, banking has become a huge business in a state formerly known only for making chemicals.

Chemical plants abound in northern Delaware.

EARNING A LIVING

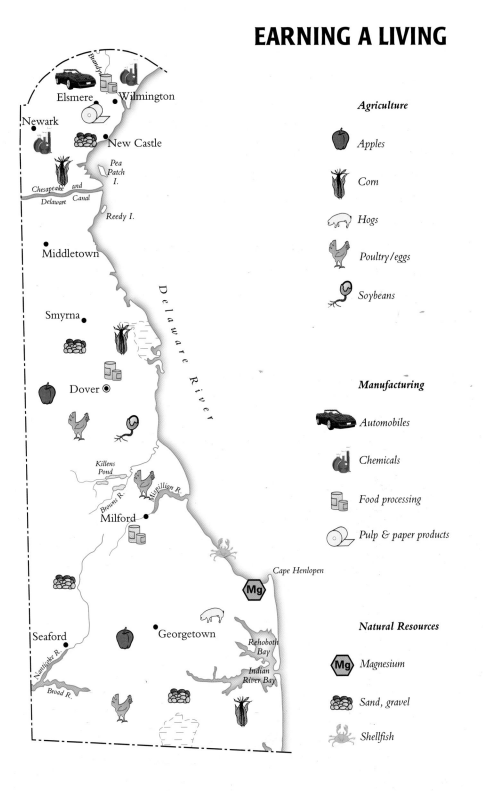

Elsmere • Wilmington

Newark

• New Castle

Pea
Patch
I.

Chesapeake and
Delaware Canal

Reedy I.

Delaware River

• Middletown

Smyrna •

Dover ◉

Killens
Pond

Misvillion R.

Brouns R.

Milford •

Cape Henlopen

Mg

Seaford

• Georgetown

Rehoboth
Bay

Indian
River Bay

Nanticoke R.

Broad R.

Agriculture

🍎 Apples

🌽 Corn

🐖 Hogs

🐓 Poultry/eggs

🌱 Soybeans

Manufacturing

🚗 Automobiles

Chemicals

Food processing

Pulp & paper products

Natural Resources

Mg Magnesium

Sand, gravel

🦀 Shellfish

LOCATION IS EVERYTHING

In addition to its banking laws, Wilmington, the state's biggest city, has something else in its favor when it comes to conducting business: its location. Journalist Norman Lockman says, "Wilmington is a very easy city to get in and out of. There is a joke that goes that Wilmington is an easy place to do business in because you can leave it so easily."

Wilmington is roughly midway between New York City and Washington, D.C. At most, it's a forty-minute drive from Philadelphia International Airport. Interstate 95, the main north–south superhighway along the East Coast, runs through downtown.

Wilmington is also one of the few American cities that relies heavily on passenger rail service. Amtrak's Metroliner, a high-speed train that can travel up to 125 miles per hour, stops at Wilmington fifteen times a day on runs to and from New York City and Wash-

GROSS STATE PRODUCT: $31.6 BILLION

(2000 estimated)

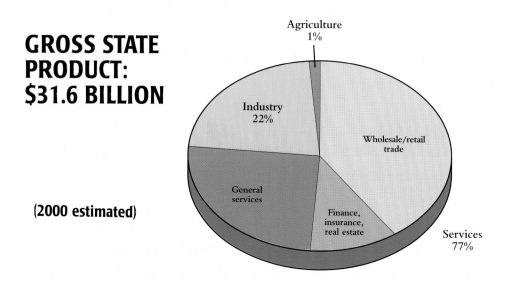

Agriculture 1%

Industry 22%

Wholesale/retail trade

General services

Finance, insurance, real estate

Services 77%

ington. Travelers can leave New York on the Metroliner and be in Wilmington in about an hour and a half. "It's very handy for people who have to do commerce here," says Lockman.

BROILERS, BEACHES, AND SEAFOOD

Most banking and chemical businesses are based in and around Wilmington. What do people do in the state's two southern counties?

Geography holds the answer. The flat land of central and southern Delaware is prime farm country. This is where Delaware's famed broiler chickens are raised.

Until the 1950s, oysters were the most sought-after catch in Delaware. A parasite in Delaware Bay ruined the business. Although some oysters are still harvested today, the people who work on Delaware's water are more likely to catch clams, fish, and crabs. Delaware crabs are regarded by seafood lovers as a true delicacy.

Delaware's seaside communities, such as Rehoboth Beach, Bethany Beach, and Dewey Beach, depend on tourists to occupy their sandy shorelines and spend money on food and lodging. So many visitors come from Washington, D.C., to Rehoboth Beach in summer that the Delaware beach town has been nicknamed the Nation's Summer Capital.

The name *Rehoboth* is from a Biblical word meaning "open spaces." That has become a bit of a joke on the Delaware seacoast, since more and more homes are being built there. Local folks like to see their area grow and prosper. But at the same time, they don't

WHICH CAME FIRST— THE CHICKEN OR THE EGG

The broiler chicken industry, one of Delaware's biggest businesses, was started by accident.

One day in the early 1920s, a farming couple named Cecile and Wilmer Steele, who lived near Ocean View, placed an order for fifty chicks. The Steeles wanted to sell eggs to make a little extra money. By mistake, they received five hundred chicks, not fifty.

Instead of returning the chicks, the Steeles raised them in a piano crate. About four months later, they sold them for a huge profit. The next year they ordered one thousand chicks, and again they made a big profit. Competing farmers saw how the Steeles were making money and decided to raise large numbers of chickens, too. By the mid-1920s, the broiler industry in Sussex County was booming. It continues to do so today.

Crabs have long been regarded as a Delaware delicacy.

want their communities to lose their low-key feel. If too many people move in, the beach towns may become just as congested as the cities newcomers moved there to escape. The question is how much development is too much.

BEYOND DU PONT

Other Delaware businesses? Automakers DaimlerChrysler and General Motors maintain plants in the northern Delaware city of Newark. Newark is also home to the University of Delaware.

One of the more unusual businesses in the state is also located

in Newark. W. L. Gore and Associates makes Gore-Tex, a fabric used in everything from dental floss to guitar strings. Gore-Tex is best known for its use in outerwear donned by skiers, hunters, and backpackers. The company was founded in 1958 by a man named Bill Gore, who had just quit working at—where else?—Du Pont.

"The sand is fine and there are not a lot of rocks," says Kevin Nielsen, a regular visitor to Delaware's beaches. The sand castle contest at Rehoboth Beach is one of many tourist lures.

4 LIFE IN DELAWARE

Unlike the brash Texas cowboy or the reserved Vermonter, there is no common stereotype of Delawareans. To some outsiders from big cities, Delawareans might seem dull. Some refer to the state as "Dull–aware." Of course, no stereotype is completely true. The real story is less cut-and-dried.

NORTH AND SOUTH

Even though Delaware is a small state, it is surprisingly diverse. In terms of its character, Delaware is almost like two states. Thanks to the Chesapeake and Delaware Canal, Delaware residents often refer to parts of their home state as "above the canal" or "below the canal."

Journalist Norman Lockman says, "As far as the north versus south mentality, Delaware is a kind of unique microcosm of the country. People above the canal tend to behave like people from Connecticut. People from the bottom part of the state tend to behave more like people from Georgia."

Above the canal are the cities of Wilmington and Newark, wealthy suburbs, and miles of industrial facilities. Even though it takes up a very small portion of the state, Delaware above the canal is home to most of the state's population.

Below the canal the only city of any significant size is Dover,

The Swedish settlers who founded Fort Christina in 1638 would be astounded by the size of today's bustling Wilmington.

whose population is a mere 30,000. The rest of Delaware below the canal is small towns, tidy villages, and beach resorts. The overwhelming majority of the land is devoted not to industry but to agriculture. The people living there tend to have a different attitude about life and politics. Lockman notes, "The bottom part of the state is conservative. The top part of the state, while not liberal by any standards, is more moderate."

The difference in views and lifestyle leads to a bit of a rivalry between those living above and below the canal. Some people living in the extreme north tend to think of downstaters as slow, backward, and closed-minded. Some in lower Delaware think of their state's northern citizens as snobs who live in a crowded, smelly, industrial area. Sussex County man Bill Collins says, "If I had my choice, we'd ship everything above the canal back to Pennsylvania."

Delaware "below the canal" has land perfect for farming.

POPULATION GROWTH: 1790–2000

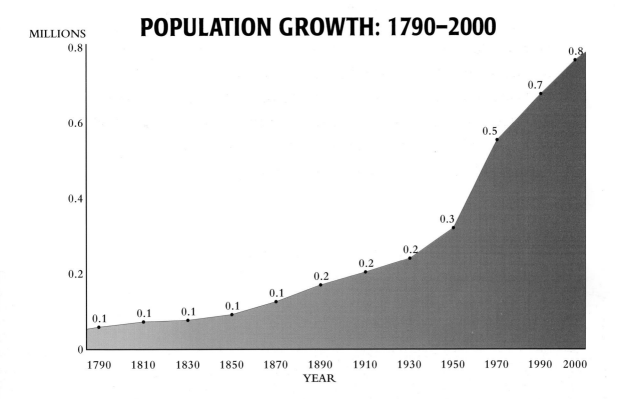

Many of these differences stem from the state's geography. The hills and waterways above the canal lent themselves to industry. The flat land of lower Delaware is ideal for farming. The canal just happened to be built in a place that perfectly divides the two parts of the state.

EARLY SETTLERS TO RECENT IMMIGRANTS

The population of Delaware has changed greatly since the Swedes, Dutch, and English battled over the land three centuries ago. Still, if you travel up and down the state and talk with the people, you

CANNOLI, PIZZA, AND MUSIC

One of Delaware's biggest festivals takes place in Wilmington in June. The setting is the grounds of St. Anthony of Padua Roman Catholic Church and the event is called St. Anthony's Festa Italiana.

In addition to carnival rides, six outdoor cafés are set up. Each serves a different type of Italian food, ranging from pizza and chicken spezzato to pastries such as cannoli. At each café a live band performs a form of Italian music. While at one café you might hear opera, your friend dining at a different café could be listening to modern popular Italian songs.

The festival began as a fund-raiser for the church and its schools in 1975. It has since grown to a mammoth event drawing more than 300,000 people over eight days. Many visitors are former Wilmington residents who moved from the city but come back every year for this one event.

will meet some whose ancestors were here hundreds of years ago.

As Wilmington grew and became a sizable port, immigrants began arriving. The first wave of immigration in the 1700s brought Scotch-Irish settlers. Over the next 150 years, scores of immigrants came from Ireland, Germany, Poland, Russia, and Italy. In the last several decades, there has been an influx of Hispanics, mostly from Puerto Rico. African Americans have been in Delaware since the early 1600s.

The vast majority of the residents of rural Kent and Sussex Counties are white. In 1996, the black population of Wilmington, in New Castle County, was more than 37,000—slightly more than half the city's population. It is also roughly equal to the African-American population of the two lower counties combined.

LIVING TOGETHER

Although race relations in Delaware have improved over the years, people still sometimes have problems there, just as they do everywhere.

George Turner is an African American who has lived in Wilmington most of his life. Turner reports that "people from bigger cities like Washington, Chicago, or Atlanta come to visit and they say '[Wilmington] is one of the most racist, prejudiced places I've ever seen.' Living here, I don't see that because I've more or less adapted to it."

According to Turner, "Racism isn't as blatant as it was years ago, but that's even more dangerous, because you don't know who's your friend and who isn't." Yet there are times when Turner is openly

Though one of the nation's smallest states, Delaware has a racially diverse population. This is a scene from an African-American festival in Dover.

reminded of his race. Once, when he was alone in an elevator, the doors opened, and a white woman was waiting to get in. Turner recalls, "I said 'Good morning,' to her and she looked at me and didn't get in. . . . It kind of ruined my whole day realizing that just being black and male made me a threat to her."

Even when people try to be helpful, there is sometimes a general lack of understanding. Asha Dodia, an Asian American from Newark who has lived in the United States since 1967, recalls a time she asked for help finding an item in a grocery store. The manager noticed her foreign accent and immediately asked for a Spanish translator. He wrongly assumed that as an immigrant, she must be from Latin America. "He didn't even give me an opportunity to ask my question," Dodia recalls.

The YWCA of New Castle County has begun a series of discussions called race study circles, where people talk over problems to try to understand other people's cultures and points of view. Most participants believe that the circles have increased their understanding of others' beliefs and attitudes. Many times, people come to realize they are blind to their own prejudices. For example, says the YWCA's Ruth Sokolowski, "Most white people don't think of checking their children before they go into a store to make sure they are not bringing in one of their own belongings. But black people do because they are concerned they might be accused of shoplifting. Those with white skin are privileged in ways they sometimes don't realize."

People of all races have entered the program believing they have no racial biases, but soon learn they too hold prejudiced opinions. Lynn Paul, who has taken part in several circles, says, "It's probably the first time in your life you can put yourself in someone else's shoes. It gives you an opportunity to listen and say, 'Oh, so that's why you feel that way.'"

AMISH AND NATIVE AMERICANS

People usually think of the Amish as living in Pennsylvania and Ohio, but about two hundred Amish families live in the country-side west of Dover.

The Amish are Protestant fundamentalists who take every word

It's surprising to many, but Delaware is home to a self-contained Amish community near Dover.

ETHNIC DELAWARE

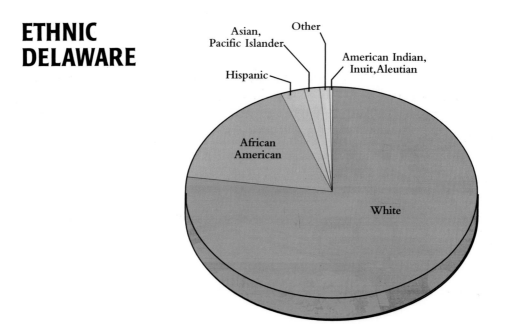

of the Bible as the absolute truth. Unlike most fundamentalists, the Amish deny themselves nearly all modern conveniences and pleasures. They own no televisions, computers, radios, washing machines, or even cars. They travel by horse and buggy. They also believe strongly in nonviolence. Because of this, they do not serve in the military.

Most Amish work as farmers. Amish children attend school only until the eighth grade. No Amish person wears bright-colored clothing, short pants, or short-sleeve shirts. Even in the heat of summer, the Amish cover up from head to toe.

You will sometimes see Amish traveling the two-lane roads of central Delaware in their buggies. On Tuesdays and Fridays of most weeks, Amish homemade foods such as sausages, baked goods, and preserves are sold at an open-air market in Dover.

PEACH COBBLER

Thanks to Delaware's many years as a peach-growing center, peach cobbler is a popular treat in the First State. Have an adult help you make this delicious dessert.

Batter ingredients:
    ½ cup sugar
    ¾ cup flour
    2 teaspoons baking powder
    salt
    ½ cup milk
Other ingredients:
    ½ stick butter
    2 cups fresh peaches, sliced
    1 cup sugar

Combine the batter ingredients. Melt the butter into a deep glass bowl. Pour the batter into the bowl. Mix 2 cups fresh sliced peaches with 1 cup sugar and pour into the batter. Do not stir at any point. Bake at 350 degrees for 1 hour. Peach cobbler can be served hot or cold. For extra fun, serve it with ice cream.

Native Americans celebrating their heritage in the First State dance at the annual Nanticoke Indian Powwow.

Like every other state, Delaware still retains a population of those who were here first. In southwestern Delaware lives a tribe of roughly five hundred Nanticoke Indians. The Nanticoke are best known to other Delawareans for the annual powwow they hold in September. At the powwow, the Native Americans demonstrate their crafts, foods, and customs to visitors of all backgrounds. Storytelling and ceremonial dancing are popular activities at the event.

5 DISTINGUISHED DELAWAREANS

Although Delaware is a small state with a small population, it has produced its share of people who have made a difference.

A RIDE INTO HISTORY

What Paul Revere is to the United States, Caesar Rodney is to Delaware. Like Revere, Rodney made a famous, frantic ride into history.

It was 1776, the most famous year in the history of the United States. The Continental Congress spent the spring and summer meeting in Philadelphia debating whether or not the colonies should declare their independence from Great Britain. In late June, the Continental Congress was about to vote on this important matter.

Delaware had three delegates to the Continental Congress. One was Thomas McKean, who favored independence. A second was George Read, who was against independence. The third was Caesar Rodney.

In 1776, Rodney was an active civil servant. In the previous twenty years, he had served as a justice of the peace, a Delaware supreme court justice, and a member of the Delaware Assembly. He also served as captain in a Delaware militia.

As June was ending, Rodney was in Delaware, not in Philadelphia where the Continental Congress was meeting. Like Thomas

American patriot Caesar Rodney is immortalized by this statue in Wilmington.

McKean, Rodney favored independence. As soon as he heard from McKean that a vote regarding independence was scheduled for July 2, Rodney made plans to be there. His ride covered a distance of eighty miles. Today, a motorist can drive that distance in a little more than an hour. That was not the case in 1776. Instead, Rodney made a mad ride on his horse through thunder and rain.

He arrived on the afternoon of July 2, just before the vote was to take place. He has been quoted as saying, "As I believe the voice of my constituents and of all sensible and honest men is in favor of independence, my own judgment concurs with them. I vote for independence."

SEARCHING FOR STARS

Annie Jump Cannon became a woman of note at the tender age of sixteen. At that time she was one of the first women from Delaware to attend college. The year was 1880 and the teenager went to class at Wellesley College in Massachusetts.

Astronomer Annie Jump Cannon was the Census Taker of the Sky.

However, it was years later when Cannon became known across the world as a skilled scientist. Called the Census Taker of the Sky, she spent years discovering and identifying stars while working at the Harvard College Observatory in Cambridge, Massachusetts.

Cannon was admired for her ability to work with incredible speed. From 1911 through 1915, she classified an average of 5,000 stars per month. It is believed that she cataloged roughly 350,000 stars in her lifetime. She is also credited with being the first astronomer to prove that most stars can be classified according to color.

Of the many honors Cannon received, probably the greatest was being the first woman to receive an honorary doctorate from the highly respected Oxford University in England. Cannon never forgot those who would come after her. In 1932, Cannon donated prize money she had won to the American Astronomical Society to start a new prize for notable women in astronomy.

Cannon was born in Dover in 1863 during the middle of the Civil War. She died in 1941, when World War II was raging in Europe. Perhaps that is why she said just before she died, "In troubled days it is good to have something outside our planet, something fine and distant for comfort."

BASEBALL HALL OF FAMER

Memorialized on a plaque in the National Baseball Hall of Fame in Cooperstown, New York, is a ballplayer named William Julius "Judy" Johnson. He is honored alongside such household names as Babe Ruth, Ty Cobb, and Joe DiMaggio. However, Judy Johnson

"Judy Johnson was the smartest third baseman I ever came across . . . and I saw Brooks Robinson, Mike Schmidt and even Pie Traynor," remembered fellow Negro Leagues ballplayer Ted Page.

From the Collection of the National Baseball Hall of Fame

was never a household name in most American homes.

From the 1880s until 1947, African Americans were excluded from playing major league baseball. Instead, they played on their own teams and formed their own leagues, known as the Negro Leagues. The Negro Leagues thrived on some of the most talented ballplayers ever to wear uniforms.

However, few people other than African Americans paid any

attention at the time. Although the first members of the National Baseball Hall of Fame were chosen in 1936, it was not until 1971 that a player from the Negro Leagues was inducted.

Delaware resident Judy Johnson was perhaps the greatest third baseman in the history of the Negro Leagues. He played from 1918 through 1937 for teams such as the Philadelphia Hilldales, the Homestead Grays, and the Pittsburgh Crawfords.

A clutch hitter and quick fielder, Johnson led the Hilldales to three straight pennants from 1923 through 1925. During those years he had batting averages of .391, .369, and .392.

Johnson made the best of playing in a segregated league. Describing the long trips from city to city to play different teams, Johnson recalled, "We would get tired from the riding. We would fuss like chickens, but when you put the uniform on, it was different. We just knew that was your job and you'd just do it. We used to have a lot of fun, and there were some bad days, too, but there was always sun shining some place."

Johnson lived long enough to see himself inducted into the hall of fame in 1975. He died in Wilmington in 1989.

BLUESMAN

The raucous sounds of guitarist George Thorogood have been entertaining rock and blues fans since December 1, 1973. That was the day he and his band, the Destroyers, first performed live. The setting was Lane Hall at the University of Delaware.

Since then George Thorogood & the Destroyers have released over a dozen albums and have performed with such blues and rock

Guitarist George Thorogood said of those who came to see him perform his blues-rock, "Let's get these people up on their feet, get them laughing and dancing. Let them know there's a good time to be had."

legends as Bo Diddley, ZZ Top, and the Rolling Stones. He has become so identified with his home state that some fans call his band the Delaware Destroyers.

Thorogood was born in Wilmington in 1950. Unlike many professional musicians, George was not interested in playing music when he was young. Then in 1970 he attended a performance of blues great John Lee Hooker. That concert ignited Thorogood's passion for music.

Thorogood and the Destroyers gained a reputation by playing small clubs not in Wilmington, but in Boston, Massachusetts, a city with a more active music scene. At first, no record label was interested in them. Their first album, *George Thorogood and the Destroyers*, was not released until 1977.

Their second album, *Move It on Over*, brought the band national recognition. The title song had first been recorded years earlier by country music immortal Hank Williams. Thorogood and the Destroyers gave the song a blues treatment, and it received heavy radio play.

Thorogood compares his band to a "burger joint." He means that his music is basic rock and roll and blues. It is not flashy or especially innovative. But, he adds, there is nothing wrong with selling cheeseburgers if they are quality cheeseburgers.

DELAWARE'S FIRST FAMILY

Several states are identified with a certain prominent family. Such families are called the "first family" of the state. One might say the first family of New York is the Rockefellers. In Massachusetts the Kennedys are the first family. In Louisiana it is the Longs.

Delaware has its own first family: the du Ponts. It is important to separate the Du Pont Company from the du Pont family. Some du Ponts still serve on the board of directors of the Du Pont Company. However, the last du Pont to serve as chairman of the board of directors was Lammot du Pont Copeland, who served until 1971. Copeland was also the last du Pont family member to serve as company president.

Aside from business, du Ponts have played leading roles in Delaware's political and cultural activities for nearly two hundred years. They have given much money to Delaware's institutions.

For instance, in the early twentieth century, three cousins, all great-grandsons of Éleuthère, were generous with their fortune. T. Coleman du Pont used his money to build a major two-lane highway from Wilmington to the Maryland border. He donated it to the government for public use. Alfred I. du Pont gave his money

According to historian Carol Hoffecker, Éleuthère Irénée du Pont was "probably a little dull. When he walked into a room, heads didn't turn. He was in no way flamboyant."

to the elderly when the state pension program broke down. Pierre Samuel du Pont donated large amounts of money to Delaware's school system.

Yet not all du Ponts have made the family proud. For years John du Pont, a great-great-grandson of the company founder, was best known for the training center for Olympic wrestlers he built in nearby Pennsylvania.

However, he later began to have severe mental health problems. In 1996, John du Pont shot to death one of the center's star wrestlers. Americans were stunned that a person from one of the nation's wealthiest families would commit such a crime. Despite his mental illness, John du Pont was found guilty of third-degree murder.

Today, the du Pont family shows no signs of losing its financial power. Every so often magazines list the five hundred wealthiest people in the United States. There are usually ten to twelve members of the du Pont family on the list.

6 SIGHTSEEING AND SUNBATHING

No one traveling through this small state will ever lack things to do. From lavish mansions to relaxing beaches, Delaware will keep any sightseer busy.

THE MANSION WITH THE STRANGEST NAME

Northern Delaware exposes visitors to soul-pleasing culture rather than mind-clearing beaches. One can thank the du Pont family for these cultural attractions. After all, they once lived in many of them.

The king of Delaware mansions is called Winterthur Museum and Gardens. Six miles northwest of Wilmington, it was the country home of Henry Francis du Pont.

The main building at Winterthur is nine stories high and contains 196 rooms. However, the mansion was much smaller when it was first built. It grew because of Henry du Pont's hobby: collecting American antiques. He began by buying rare furniture. Then he went on to purchase entire rooms full of early American furnishings. There was one problem however: where would he keep all his treasures?

The answer was to build additions to the house. Today, Winterthur houses the world's largest collection of American decorative arts. A few examples of what visitors can see are a dinner service

PLACES TO SEE

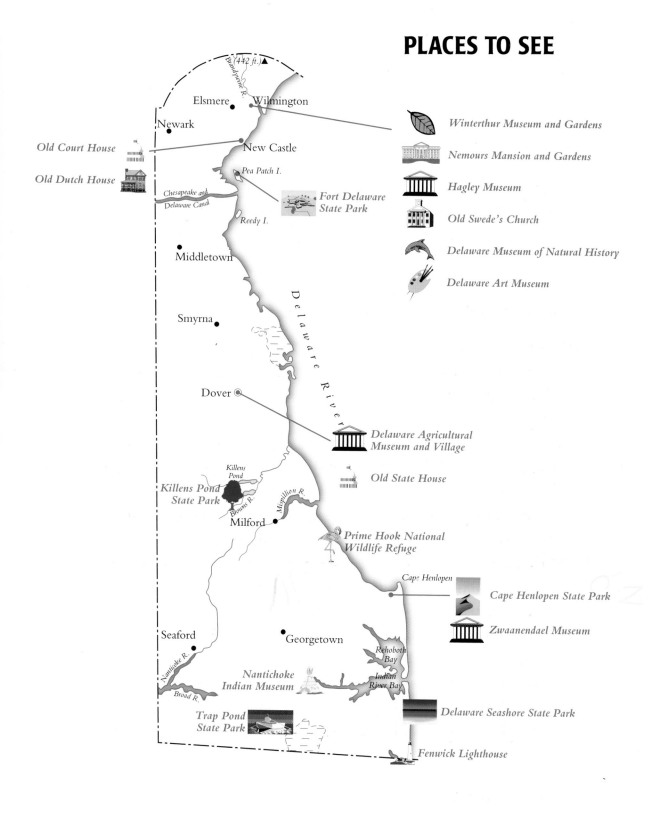

(442 ft.) ▲

Brandywine R.

Elsmere   Wilmington

Newark

Old Court House

New Castle

Old Dutch House

Pea Patch I.

Chesapeake and
Delaware Canal

Reedy I.

Fort Delaware
State Park

Middletown

Delaware River

Smyrna

Dover

Delaware Agricultural
Museum and Village

Killens
Pond

Old State House

Killens Pond
State Park

Brouns R.

Mispillion R.

Milford

Prime Hook National
Wildlife Refuge

Cape Henlopen

Cape Henlopen State Park

Zwaanendael Museum

Seaford

Georgetown

Rehoboth
Bay

Nantichoke
Indian Museum

Indian
River Bay

Nanticoke R.

Broad R.

Trap Pond
State Park

Delaware Seashore State Park

Fenwick Lighthouse

Winterthur Museum and Gardens

Nemours Mansion and Gardens

Hagley Museum

Old Swede's Church

Delaware Museum of Natural History

Delaware Art Museum

Winterthur, which boasts nearly two hundred rooms, is one of the grandest homes in America.

made for George Washington, an entire room from Massachusetts dating to the 1600s, and silver tankards crafted by the famous patriot Paul Revere.

Winterthur's sights are not limited to the indoors. Outside are lush gardens and wooded paths where visitors can take relaxing strolls.

Winterthur hosts special events throughout the year. Among the biggest is a Sunday in May filled with horse races. The day's highlights are the steeplechase races, where horses jump over hedges and fences. There are also pony races and a parade of antique carriages.

How did Winterthur get its unusual name? The mansion was originally built in 1839 by Evelina Gabrielle du Pont and her husband, James Antoine Bidermann. Bidermann named his new home for the city of Winterthur, Switzerland, where his ancestors had lived. When Henry Francis du Pont inherited the home in 1927, he kept the name.

MORE HOMES OF THE RICH AND FAMOUS

Henry Francis was not the only du Pont to leave a fascinating legacy to the people of Delaware. Another plush residence open to the public is Nemours Mansion and Gardens. It is named for the du Pont family's ancestral home in France.

To say that Nemours is smaller than Winterthur is like saying that Sammy Sosa is not as good a home run hitter as Mark McGwire. Nemours contains 102 rooms and sits on three hundred acres. Inside the main mansion are priceless works of art, fine European tapestries, and antique furniture.

As at Winterthur, an added bonus for visitors are the lush gardens. Alfred I. du Pont, who built Nemours, based his gardens on the formal gardens that surround French palaces.

Although these du Pont mansions lure admirers of antiques and gardens, another du Pont property draws history buffs. Despite its name, Hagley Museum, just north of Wilmington, is much more than just a museum. It is called the place "where the du Pont story begins." Located in the woods high on the banks of Brandywine Creek, the grounds of Hagley Museum include the first du Pont mansion, built by Éleuthère Irénée du Pont, who founded the du Pont powder works. This mansion was built in 1803.

What makes Hagley different from the other du Pont estates are the historic buildings on the grounds. Du Pont's original gunpowder mills are preserved. An 1814 cotton mill shares the grounds with a working 1870s machine shop. At a spot called Blacksmith Hill are buildings depicting how mill workers lived 140 years ago. There's even a period school restored with attached wooden desks, rows of quill pens, and small slate chalkboards.

AWAY FROM THE DU PONTS

Of course, not every historic site in Wilmington is connected to the du Ponts. One of the oldest Protestant churches still in use in North America sits on the outskirts of downtown. It is officially called the Holy Trinity Episcopal Church, although locals refer to it as the Old Swedes Church. The stone church was built in 1698 by a Swedish congregation. Close by is the Hendrickson House, a stone farmhouse built in 1690 in Pennsylvania but moved to this location.

Within walking distance of the Old Swedes Church is the Kalmar Nyckel Shipyard Museum. The *Kalmar Nyckel* was the boat that brought the first Swedish settlers to Delaware in 1638. The museum

The gardens at Nemours Mansion stretch for a third of a mile.

tells about that first landing along with the history of shipbuilding in the region.

No tour of Wilmington is complete without a stop at Rodney Square. The downtown square was named in memory of the patriot who made the famous ride to Philadelphia in 1776. Its centerpiece is a statue of Rodney on horseback.

Wilmington also has its share of quality museums. Inside the Delaware Museum of Natural History are more than one hundred displays, including dioramas of African animals and extinct birds in their natural habitats. Some of the favorite exhibits are a recreation of Australia's Great Barrier Reef and a massive shell collection.

The Delaware Art Museum is best known for its collection of American art, including works by painters Howard Pyle, Winslow Homer, and Maxfield Parrish. Other respected Wilmington museums are the Delaware History Museum, which is housed in a former Woolworth's department store, and the Delaware Toy & Miniature Museum.

NEW CASTLE AND BEYOND

New Castle was once described in *American Heritage* magazine as possibly "the closest thing to a ghost town on the East Coast." This does not mean that New Castle is similar to the abandoned towns of the Old West. After all, nearly five thousand people live in New Castle. It means that New Castle is a beautifully preserved historic town. Although it is located just two miles south of the Delaware Memorial Bridge and busy Interstate 295, it looks much as it did two hundred years ago.

TEN LARGEST CITIES

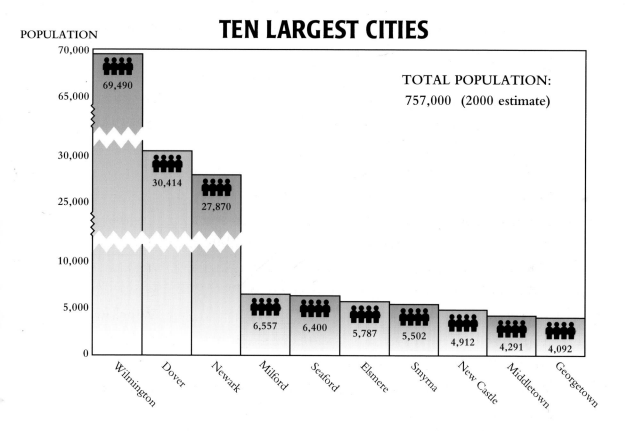

TOTAL POPULATION:
757,000 (2000 estimate)

70,000
69,490

65,000

30,000
30,414

27,870

25,000

10,000

5,000
6,557   6,400   5,787   5,502   4,912   4,291   4,092

0

Wilmington Dover Newark Milford Seaford Elsmere Smyrna New Castle Middletown Georgetown

Why is New Castle so well preserved? In the late 1700s, the town was an important stop on a stagecoach route connecting Philadelphia, Annapolis, and Baltimore. However, by the mid-1800s, Philadelphia and Baltimore were taking shape as the region's biggest cities. So new roads and railroad lines were built to directly connect those two major cities, and New Castle was bypassed. Because New Castle was no longer an important stopping point for travelers, there was little reason to construct new buildings. New Castle's old ones have never been torn down.

Most of the structures in New Castle are made from brick. They include the Old Court House, which was built in 1732. The four flags on the balcony are from Sweden, the Netherlands, Great Britain, and the United States, all nations that have governed New Castle at some point in history.

Along Third Street is a group of brick houses dating to Delaware's early days. One, a small home with a steeply pitched

Old brick buildings line many streets in New Castle.

In spite of this moat, some of the 12,500 Confederate prisoners who lived at Fort Delaware escaped during the Civil War. However, nearly 2,700 inmates died from disease.

roof, is called the Old Dutch House and was built in the late 1600s. This modest house is the oldest in New Castle, and it is believed to be the oldest in the entire state.

Probably Delaware's most famous historic building outside

Wilmington is in Fort Delaware State Park. The park is located on Pea Patch Island in the Delaware River. The only way to get there is by boat.

On the island is a fort that housed Confederate prisoners of war during the Civil War. This five-sided structure has huge, solid granite walls. A moat surrounds it. Despite the massive walls and moat, some prisoners escaped and were sheltered by supporters of the Confederacy in Delaware and Maryland.

People once risked their lives to escape the fort, but today they pay to visit it. Inside are exhibits relating to the Civil War. Travelers also come to Pea Patch Island to walk its many nature trails. Wading birds such as herons and egrets find the island an inviting place to make their nests. An observation tower helps visitors spot the birds. Some people just enjoy the boat ride around Pea Patch Island. Sunset cruises are offered on summer evenings.

DELAWARE'S WILD SIDE

Not every site in northern Delaware is about history. Lums Pond State Park, located just above the canal, is built around the largest freshwater pond in the state. It is an ideal spot for boaters, and you can rent sailboats, rowboats, pedal boats, and canoes. One of the park's unusual features is the Sensory Trail, which encourages walkers to use all their senses rather than just sight. There are also trails for biking, horseback riding, hiking, and snowmobiling.

Fox Point State Park is a newly developed park tucked in amid the buildings and highways of the Wilmington metropolitan area. Located along the banks of the Delaware River, the park lures people wanting a green and open place to ride their bicycles, have a picnic, or play a game of horseshoes.

CAPITAL ATTRACTIONS

The state capital, Dover, is home to some noted museums. The Delaware Agricultural Museum and Village might have a boring name, but it is more than a collection of old tractors and farm tools. It is the place to visit a barbershop, a one-room schoolhouse, a

At the Delaware Agricultural Museum, farm vehicles are powered the old-fashioned way.

store, and a train station frozen in the late 1800s. A "Farmer's Christmas" is celebrated here in early December with period music and crafts.

One of Dover's more unusual museums is the Johnson Victrola Museum. Victrola was the brand name of the first record players, the ancestors of today's compact disc players. The museum is in Dover because the company founder, Eldridge Reeves Johnson, was born there. Step inside the building to see record players from the late 1800s and early 1900s. You can also visit a recreated 1920s Victrola dealer's store.

Dover's second-largest employer after the state government is Dover Air Force Base. The base is the largest in the East. It is not unusual to see the C-5 Galaxy, the biggest airplane in the country, zooming through the skies above Dover. Though unauthorized visitors cannot enter the base, they are allowed to visit the base's museum. It houses aircraft dating back to World War II.

Dover residents who want to cool off sometimes head south to Killens Pond State Park, which includes a water park, complete with water slides and pools. Those searching for more peaceful activities can take a narrated pontoon boat tour of Killens Pond. The park's hiking trails include Ice Storm Trail, which gives visitors a chance to observe the forest's recovery from harsh ice storms that hit the park in 1994.

RESORTS RULE

Southern Delaware is the vacation destination for people who care little about history and museums. This is the land where beach

The boardwalk at Rehoboth Beach is a great place for people watching, or just stretching out with a good book.

resorts rule. It is popular with those who wish to do nothing more than stretch out on the sand and relax.

The busiest beach town is Rehoboth Beach. This seaside setting was first developed in 1873 by Methodist church leaders. They were looking for a quiet place to hold religious summer camp meetings.

Nobody can describe Rehoboth Beach today as quiet—at least not in summer. In winter, the population of the community is a little over 1,200. But on a hot summer day, it may swell to a crushing 50,000. Aside from the sun and sand, tourists admire the town's many one-hundred-year-old homes on tree-lined streets.

Farther south, near the Maryland border, are Bethany Beach and Fenwick Island. They are promoted as Delaware's "quiet resorts." Both are mainly residential. They don't have the large hotels one finds at Rehoboth Beach. Delaware Secretary of Agriculture Jack Tarburton bought a vacation home in this part of the state. What he says he loves best is "the solitude—the only commerce in town is one phone booth, and the scenery changes every day."

Delaware's northernmost beach resort is the town of Lewes (pronounced "LEW–is"), which hugs the eastern edge of Cape Henlopen. Lewes offers proof that even at the beach Delaware visitors cannot escape history. It was near here in 1631 that the Dutch founded the settlement they called Zwaanendael.

Today, visitors can explore the Zwaanendael Museum. The museum building is a replica of a Dutch town hall. Inside are military and maritime relics and the remains of a Dutch ship that sank in 1798.

Like New Castle, Lewes has a collection of preserved old homes to be visited. They include a nineteenth-century country store and an 1850 doctor's office. Aside from history and beaches, Lewes is also known for its fine boutique and antique shopping.

Visitors can stretch their legs at Cape Henlopen State Park, home of the highest sand dune between Cape Cod in Massachusetts and Cape Hatteras in North Carolina. Known as the Great Dune, it rises eighty feet above the coastline. People can also exercise their legs in an observation tower built during World War II. Those who climb the 115 steps to the top are rewarded with a spectacular view.

Zwaanendael offers a bit of Holland in Delaware, U.S.A.

Those searching for outdoor fun in the southern reaches of the state can go boating among the bald cypress trees at Trap Pond State Park. Others might wish to paddle a canoe or stroll the trails at Prime Hook National Wildlife Refuge, a haven for Delaware's birds and other animals.

Southern Delaware is home to the Nanticoke Indians, most of whom live near Millsboro. The Nanticoke Indian Museum is located in a restored schoolhouse and displays Native American pottery, beadwork, baskets, ancient arrowheads, and other tools.

ECO-TOURISM IN DELAWARE

A current trend in travel is "eco-tourism," which is short for ecology tourism. This is travel that is based on experiencing nature and helping the environment.

A visitors' guide to southern Delaware describes the difference between a tourist and an eco-traveler: "A tourist sits on the beach all day hoping for a suntan. An eco-traveler walks the beach in search of clues to Delaware's marine environment. He or she may take a guided tour, participate in a sea-going classroom activity or stalk the salt marshes for a glimpse of a rare bird."

Many people think that eco-tourism takes place mainly in national parks or in the rain forests of tropical countries. However, Delaware is filled with opportunities for the eco-tourist. Since the state sits along the Atlantic flyway, migrating birds fly by or stop. The best time for bird-watching is spring and early summer when horseshoe crabs lay their eggs on the beach. For shorebirds, the eggs are like ice cream is to a kid.

Every October, the University of Delaware hosts a Coastal Clean-Up and Coast Day near Lewes. Other eco-tourist activities include canoeing down the Nanticoke River and whale and dolphin watching. Visitors who take part in activities such as these leave with more than a suntan. They gain a deeper understanding of Delaware's wildlife and natural resources.

A bit of mist doesn't stop two boys from exploring Trap Pond near Laurel.

The more you see of Delaware, the more you'll realize that you shouldn't let its size mislead you. There is a lot to do within its narrow borders.

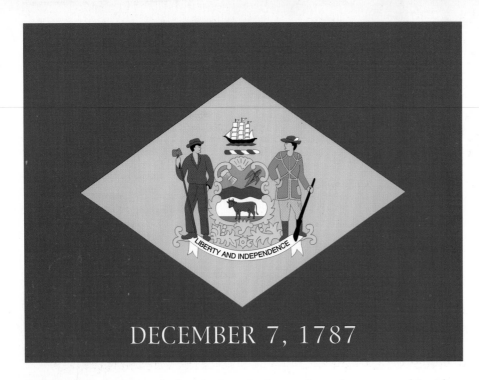

DECEMBER 7, 1787

THE FLAG: Delaware's flag depicts the image from the state seal inside a buff-colored diamond against a blue background. December 7, 1787, the day Delaware became the first state, appears below the diamond. The flag was adopted in 1913.

THE SEAL: In the middle of the state seal, which was first adopted in 1777, a farmer and a soldier support a shield. The shield shows corn, wheat, and an ox, all of which symbolize agriculture. Above the shield is a sailing ship, representing New Castle County's shipbuilding industry.

STATE SURVEY

Statehood: December 7, 1787

Origin of Name: From Delaware Bay, which was named in honor of Lord De La Warr, the governor of the Virginia Colony.

Nickname: First State

Capital: Dover

Motto: Liberty and Independence

Bird: Blue hen chicken

Flower: Peach blossom

Tree: American holly

Fish: Weakfish

Bug: Ladybug

Mineral: Sillimanite

Colors: Colonial blue and buff

Peach blossom

Ladybug

OUR DELAWARE

The official song of the First State was adopted by the state legislature in 1925.

Words by Geo. B. Hynson   **Music by Will. M. S. Brown**

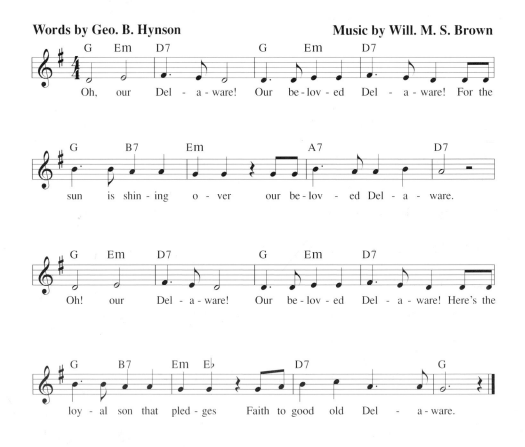

Oh, our Del – a - ware! Our be - lov - ed Del – a - ware! For the sun is shin - ing o - ver our be - lov – ed Del – a - ware.

Oh! our Del – a - ware! Our be - lov - ed Del – a - ware! Here's the loy - al son that pled - ges Faith to good old Del – a - ware.

GEOGRAPHY

Highest Point: 442 feet above sea level, on Ebright Road in New Castle County

Lowest Point: sea level along the coast

Area: 2,026 square miles

Greatest Distance, North to South: 96 miles

Greatest Distance, East to West: 39 miles

Bordering States: New Jersey to the east, Pennsylvania to the north, Maryland to the south and west

Hottest Recorded Temperature: 110°F in Millsboro on July 21, 1930

Coldest Recorded Temperature: −17°F in Millsboro on January 17, 1893

Average Annual Precipitation: 45 inches

Major Rivers: Brandywine, Broadkill, Christina, Delaware, Indian, Mispillion, Murderkill, Nanticoke, Smyrna, St. Jones

Major Lakes: Hoopes, Lums, Noxontown, Red Mill, Silver

Trees: bald cypress, beech, black tupelo, hickory, holly, loblolly pine, magnolia, oak, sassafras, sweet gum

Wild Plants: azalea, blueberry, cranberry, crocus, floating heart, hibiscus, honeysuckle, lady's slipper, violet, water lily

Animals: beaver, deer, gray fox, mink, muskrat, otter, rabbit, red fox, snapping turtle

Rabbit

Birds: blue heron, cardinal, duck, finch, grackle, hawk, oriole, sandpiper, snowy egret, teal, woodpecker, wren

Fish: bass, carp, catfish, clam, eel, oyster, porgie, rockfish, shad, trout, white perch

Endangered Animals: American peregrine falcon, bald eagle, bog turtle, Delmarva Peninsula fox squirrel, piping plover

Bog turtle

Endangered Plants: Canby's dropwort, Knieskern's beaked rush, small whorled pogonia, swamp pink

TIMELINE

Delaware History

1500s The Leni-Lenape and Nanticoke Indians live in present-day Delaware

1609 Englishman Henry Hudson enters Delaware Bay while sailing for the Dutch, becoming the first European to visit the region

1610 Samuel Argall of the Virginia Colony visits the bay and names it De La Warr Bay, after Virginia's governor

1631 The Dutch found Zwaanendael at present-day Lewes, Delaware's first European settlement, but it is destroyed within a year

1638 Swedish colonists found Fort Christina, Delaware's first permanent European settlement

1651 The Dutch take control of the region

1664 England seizes control of Delaware

1682 Pennsylvania founder William Penn is given Delaware

1704 Delaware's first legislature separate from Pennyslvania's meets

1754 Delaware's first library is established in Wilmington

1769 Newark Academy, which later became the University of Delaware, is founded

1775 The American Revolution begins

1777 Dover becomes Delaware's capital

1785 Delaware's first successful newspaper, the *Delaware Gazette*, begins publication

1787 Delaware becomes the first state

1802 Éleuthère Irénée du Pont establishes a powder mill on the banks of Brandywine Creek, marking the beginning of the du Pont empire

1829 The Chesapeake and Delaware Canal opens; Delaware establishes a system of public schools

1861–1865 Delaware fights for the Union during the Civil War

1897 Delaware adopts its fourth and present constitution

1907 The Du Pont Company is sued under the Sherman Anti-Trust Act. It is eventually forced to give up much of its explosives business

1917–1918 About 10,000 Delawareans fight in World War I

1922 Delaware's first radio station, WDEL, begins broadcasting in Wilmington

1938 The Du Pont Company develops nylon

1939–1945 World War II

1951 The Delaware Memorial Bridge opens across the Delaware River, connecting Delaware and New Jersey

1971 The state legislature passes the Coastal Zone Act, banning construction of industrial plants along the state's coastline

1981 Delaware enacts the Financial Center Development Act, which encourages out-of-state banks to move some of their operations to Delaware

1987 Delaware celebrates its 200th birthday

ECONOMY

Agricultural Products: apples, cattle, corn, greenhouse and nursery products, hay, hogs, potatoes, poultry, soybeans

Soybeans

Manufactured Products: apparel, chemicals, food products, luggage, medical supplies, nylon, transportation equipment

Natural Resources: granite, magnesium, sand and gravel, shellfish

Business and Trade: banking, insurance, real estate, tourism, wholesale and retail trade

CALENDAR OF CELEBRATIONS

Great Delaware Kite Festival Hundreds of colorful kites soar high in the sky at this event marking the beginning of spring. It takes place the Friday before Easter at Cape Henlopen State Park near Lewes.

Wilmington Garden Day Many lovely gardens and houses in the Wilmington area are open for touring the first Saturday in May.

Old Dover Days Dover celebrates its rich history each May with crafts exhibits and tours of historic homes.

Old Dover Days

Italian Festival Each June, 300,000 people descend on Wilmington to feast on rich Italian food such as spezzato, cannolis, and muffuletta while Italian music wafts through the air. A carnival and fireworks display add to the fun.

Separation Day In June, New Castle marks Delaware's declaration of independence from Great Britain with music, fireworks, and a parade of boats.

Old-Fashioned Ice Cream Festival Sampling as many flavors of ice cream as possible is the centerpiece of this July event in Wilmington. Other activities, such as demonstrations of old-fashioned hand-cranked organs, recreate the atmosphere of a festival in the late 1800s.

Delaware State Fair Each July in Harrington, Delaware hosts an old-fashioned state fair, complete with livestock competitions, carnival rides, games, concerts, delicious homemade breads, jams, and other treats, and a variety of other fun activities.

Nanticoke Indian Powwow Native Americans from up and down the East Coast travel to Millsboro in September for this celebration of Native American culture. The event includes ceremonial dances, storytelling, and Indian foods and crafts.

Delaware Nature Society Harvest Moon Festival Hayrides, pony rides, freshly pressed cider, nature walks, music, games, and arts and crafts are all part of this traditional event in Hockessin in October.

Coast Day Each October the University of Delaware in Lewes opens its facilities and research ship to the public. Films, demonstrations, and exhibits all help to educate visitors about Delaware's coastal environment.

Sea Witch Halloween and Fiddlers Festival Rehoboth Beach cuts loose for this fun-filled festival of all things spooky in October. You can tiptoe through a haunted house, relax on a horse-drawn hayride, and watch an antique car show. You'll surely want to participate in the wild costume contest—there's also one for your pet—and maybe even the broom-tossing contest.

Yuletide at Winterthur During the holiday season, several of this Wilmington mansion's rooms are decked out in traditional holiday decorations.

STATE STARS

Richard Allen (1760–1831) founded the African Methodist Episcopal Church, the first black religious denomination in the United States. Allen was born a slave in Philadelphia and grew up on a plantation in Delaware. He eventually bought his freedom and became a Methodist minister. Allen ultimately concluded that because of racism, blacks needed to form their own churches. As a result, in 1816 he established the African Methodist Episcopal Church.

Richard Allen

Henry Seidel Canby (1878–1961) was an editor who played an important role in increasing the number of people who read American literature.

Canby was the first professor at Yale University to specialize in American literature. Later, he founded the *Saturday Review of Literature*, the leading literary weekly of the 1920s and 1930s. He was also the first chairman of the board of the Book-of-the-Month Club. Canby grew up in Wilmington.

Annie Jump Cannon (1863–1941), a native of Dover, was an astronomer who developed a system for classifying stars. While working at Harvard College Observatory, she used this system to compile a catalog of 350,000 stars and similar heavenly bodies, which is still standard today. She is credited with discovering hundreds of stars. Cannon was also the first woman to receive an honorary doctorate from Oxford University in England.

Wallace Hume Carothers (1896–1937) was a chemist who developed nylon while working for Delaware's Du Pont Company. Carothers, a native of Iowa, earned his Ph.D. in 1924 and soon began teaching chemistry at Harvard. Because of his reputation as a brilliant researcher, in 1928 Du Pont hired him to head its research program. His work there led to the production of the world's first synthetic fiber, nylon.

Felix Darley (1822–1888) was the leading book illustrator of his time. From the 1840s until his death, any book that said "illustrated by Darley" was automatically a big seller. During his career, he illustrated such classics as Washington Irving's *Legend of Sleepy Hollow* and James Fenimore Cooper's *The Deerslayer*. Darley was born in Philadelphia and moved to Claymont, Delaware, after he married.

Éleuthère Irénée du Pont (1771–1834) launched one of America's most successful business empires when he founded a gunpowder mill on the banks of the Brandywine River near Wilmington. Du Pont had been born into a wealthy family in Paris and immigrated to the United States in 1799.

Oliver Evans (1755–1819) was an inventor born in Newport. As a young man working in a flour mill, he invented the grain elevator and other milling machinery, creating a fully automated mill that took just one person to run. He also built one of the first high-pressure steam engines. This vastly improved the milling process, which until then had been powered by waterwheels. Evans also invented what was likely America's first self-propelled vehicle for ground travel.

Oliver Evans

Thomas Garrett (1789–1871) was a leading abolitionist in Wilmington, who helped 2,700 people escape slavery. Garrett's house in Wilmington was an important refuge for slaves fleeing north on the Underground Railroad. In 1848, Garrett was convicted of helping slaves escape and had to sell all his property to pay the fine.

Thomas Garrett

Dallas Green

Dallas Green (1934–   ), a baseball manager, led the Philadelphia Phillies to a World Series victory in 1980. Green began his career as a pitcher with the Phillies in the early 1960s. He later managed some Phillie farm clubs before becoming manager of the major league team in 1979. Green has also worked for the Chicago Cubs, the New York Yankees, and the New York Mets. He was born in Newport.

Henry Heimlich (1920–   ) is a doctor who gained fame for developing the Heimlich maneuver, a method of saving someone who is choking. Through the 1960s, choking was a leading cause of accidental death in the United States. Heimlich realized that if a patient was squeezed, air would be forced out of his or her lungs. This often dislodged the object on which the person was choking. After Heimlich published a study on the maneuver in 1974, lives were saved using it, and Heimlich and his maneuver became well known. In the following years, the number of deaths from choking dropped dramatically. Heimlich was born in Wilmington.

Eldridge Reeves Johnson (1867–1945) was a Wilmington native who made records and record players affordable to the average American. In 1901, Johnson founded the Victor Talking Machine Company. He soon developed a way of improving the sound quality of recorded discs and designed a machine that could duplicate the records more easily. The next year he produced more than a million discs. His company eventually became the Radio Corporation of America, or RCA.

Julius "Judy" Johnson (1899–1989), a star third baseman in the Negro Leagues, was born in Wilmington. Johnson was a great hitter, with an estimated lifetime batting average of .344. After he retired, he worked as a scout for the Atlanta Braves and the Philadelphia Phillies, bringing many young black players to the major leagues. Johnson was inducted into the National Baseball Hall of Fame in 1975.

Thomas Macdonough (1783–1825) was a naval hero who was born in the Trap, which is now called Macdonough. He earned the nickname Hero of Lake Champlain after his American troops captured the entire British fleet in the Battle of Plattsburgh during the War of 1812.

Thomas Macdonough

Daniel Nathans (1928–   ) shared the 1978 Nobel Prize in medicine for his research in genetics. Nathans's work on restriction enzymes paved the way for the development of artificial hormones. Nathans was born in Wilmington.

Howard Pyle (1853–1911), who was born in Wilmington, was an illustrator, famed for his bold lines and fertile imagination. His work in *Harper's Weekly* established his reputation. He later created classic illustrations for such books as *The Merry Adventures of Robin Hood*. Pyle was also an influential teacher, helping develop the talents of such artists as Maxfield Parrish and N. C. Wyeth. After teaching elsewhere, in 1900 he founded the Howard Pyle School of Art in Wilmington, which provided illustration classes free of charge.

Howard Pyle

Jay Saunders Redding (1906–1988), a native of Wilmington, was an important literary critic and historian. His first book, *To Make a Poet Black*, published in 1939, was the first serious work about early African-American literature written by an African American. One of his most highly regarded books was *No Day of Triumph*, an angry, honest work that mixes autobiography with a discussion of black life in the South.

Estelle Taylor (1899–1958) was a beautiful movie star of the silent era. She appeared in such classics as *The Ten Commandments* and *Don Juan*. For a time she was married to boxer Jack Dempsey. Taylor was born in Wilmington.

Estelle Taylor

George Thorogood (1951–   ), a blues-rock musician from Wilmington, has attracted legions of fans through his exuberant live shows. Thorogood and his band, the Destroyers, have had such hits as "Bad to the Bone" and "Move It on Over."

TOUR THE STATE

Fort Delaware State Park (Delaware City) This fort, located on Pea Patch Island in the Delaware River, housed Confederate prisoners during the Civil War. Today, you can tour the dark cells where the prisoners were held. On a brighter note, the park also includes nature trails and a lively colony of shorebirds.

Old Dutch House (New Castle) Likely the oldest dwelling in Delaware, this house is furnished as it would have been in Dutch colonial times.

Bombay Hook National Wildlife Refuge (Smyrna) Trails and observation towers make this an excellent place to spot wildlife. The refuge is home to bald eagles, deer, shorebirds, and other creatures. The best time to visit is spring and fall, when thousands of migrating duck, snow geese, and other waterfowl stop there to feed.

Delaware Art Museum (Wilmington) This museum has a fine collection of paintings by American artists such as Winslow Homer and Edward Hopper.

Old Swedes Church (Wilmington) Built in 1698, this is one of the oldest churches in the United States. It is renowned for its beautiful black walnut pulpit.

Hagley Museum (Wilmington) At this sight, you can visit the powder mill that was the beginning of the du Pont empire, along with later factories, the first du Pont mansion in Delaware, and a collection of antique wagons.

Nemours Mansion (Wilmington) This sprawling du Pont mansion was built in 1910 and modeled after the family estate in France. It is famous for its 300-acre formal garden.

Winterthur (Wilmington) Another du Pont house, Winterthur, grew from a 12-room residence to a gigantic museum that houses the nation's finest collection of early American decorative arts. Each of its nearly 200 rooms displays a specific decorative style.

Corbit-Sharp House (Odessa) This beautifully preserved home was built in 1772. Much of the furniture in it belonged to its original owner.

Delaware Agricultural Museum and Village (Dover) Besides admiring antique farm equipment, you can also visit an old-time barbershop, schoolhouse, sawmill, blacksmith shop, and other historic buildings.

Old State House (Dover) Constructed in 1792, this is the second-oldest statehouse in continuous use in the United States. You can tour the restored chambers and view historical artifacts.

Johnson Victrola Museum (Dover) Step back in time at this museum, which looks like a music store from the 1920s. Wind-up record players, early jukeboxes, and old recordings document the early history of recorded music.

Air Mobility Command Museum (Dover) Vintage aircraft is on display at this museum on the Dover Air Force Base, but the best time to visit is during open house days, when kids can climb into the cockpit of the C-5 Galaxy, the largest American aircraft.

Delaware Seashore State Park (Rehoboth Beach) This peaceful site on Rehoboth Bay allows both ocean and bay swimming. It's also an ideal spot for fishing, clamming, surfing, and sunbathing.

Fenwick Island Lighthouse (Fenwick Island) This historic lighthouse has been warning ships of the shore since 1859.

Fenwick Island Lighthouse

Nanticoke Indian Museum (Millsboro) Ancient tools, weapons, and other artifacts educate visitors about how Delaware's Native Americans once lived.

Trap Pond State Park (Laurel) With both swampland and a large pond, this park is the perfect place to hike, bike, canoe, and picnic. During a visit to the park, you might see magnificent bald cypress trees, dazzling wildflowers, and a whole array of birds, from hummingbirds to great blue herons.

Cape Henlopen State Park (Lewes) Beautiful beaches and the biggest sand dunes in the Mid-Atlantic region are the highlights of this park.

FUN FACTS

Delaware became the first state when it ratified the Constitution on December 7, 1787.

The United States' first beauty contest was held in Rehoboth Beach in 1880. One of the three judges was the renowned inventor Thomas Edison.

Nylon was invented by researchers at the Du Pont Company in 1938.

The Delaware–Maryland border passes through the towns of Marydel and Delmar, both of which got their names by combining parts of the two state names.

Although Delaware is one of the smallest states, because of its business-friendly laws, more than half of the nation's 500 largest corporations are officially located there, even though they carry on virtually none of their business in the state.

FIND OUT MORE

Do you want to learn more about Delaware? Here are some suggestions for places to start.

GENERAL STATE BOOKS

Aylesworth, Thomas. *Mid-Atlantic States*. Broomall, PA: Chelsea House, 1996.

Brown, Dottie. *Delaware* (Hello U.S.A. series). Minneapolis: Lerner Publications, 1994.

Thompson, Kathleen. *Delaware* (Portrait of America series). Chicago: Raintree Publishers, 1996.

BOOKS ABOUT DELAWARE PEOPLE, PLACES, AND HISTORY

Asimov, Isaac, and Elizabeth Kaplan. *Henry Hudson: Arctic Explorer and North American Adventurer*. Milwaukee, WI: Gareth Stevens Children's Books, 1991.

Bierhorst, John. *The White Deer and Other Stories Told by the Lenape*. New York: William Morrow and Company, 1995.

Fenimore, Harvey Curtis, Jr. *Mike and Marnie Learn about Delaware's Beginnings: The Earliest Settlers.* Dover, DE: Finmere Books, 1994.

―――. *Mike and Marnie Learn about Delaware's Indians.* Dover, DE: Dover Post Co., 1990.

―――. *Mike and Marnie Learn about Delaware's Symbols, Slogan, Name, and Nicknames.* Dover, DE: Dover Post Co., 1990.

Marsh, Carole. *Delaware's Most Devastating Disasters and Most Calamitous Catastrophes.* Decatur, GA: Gallopade Publishing Group, 1990.

Miller, Jay. *The Delaware.* Chicago: Children's Press, 1994.

Mitchell, Barbara. *Red Bird.* New York: Lothrop, Lee & Shepard, 1996.

Wilker, John. *The Lenape Indians.* New York: Chelsea House, 1994.

Wilson, W. Emerson. *Fort Delaware.* Newark, DE: University of Delaware Press, 1986.

WEBSITES

Delaware home page: http://www.state.de.us

Delaware online news and information: http://www.newszap.com

VIDEOTAPES

Celebrate the First State. Produced by WHYY, 1987.

INDEX

Page numbers for charts, graphs, and illustrations are in boldface.